A Spoonful of Sugar

The Story of the Upjohn Pharmacy in Disneyland

Stephen Hall, MA

Interior design and layout by Nancy Levey-Bossert

Cover Design by Beach Design

Edited by Michelle Orwin

Copy Edited by Diane Hodges

Index by Connie Binder

Set in Elido, Adobe Caslon Pro, Lush Script and Slack Casual used courtesy of Adobe Typekit,
New Press Eroded by Galdino Otten

Printed in Korea

First Edition: 2025

ISBN: 9798992564501

Library of Congress Control Number: 2025932608

please visit theoldmillpress.com

This book is dedicated to my wife, Amanda, and our family.

Thank you for loving me.

It is also dedicated to my mentor Richard Wiedhopf.

Thank you for believing in me.

Table of Contents

Foreword

A visit to Disneyland and the Magic Kingdom often highlighted my family's annual trip to Palm Springs. We loved the Jungle Cruise, driving the cars in Tomorrowland, and screaming around the Matterhorn—especially when a mountaineer was climbing to the top. However, nothing brought us pride and joy like the visit to Main Street, U.S.A., and the period replica of a small-town pharmacy presented by The Upjohn Company. My mother's grandfather, Dr. W. E. Upjohn, founded The Upjohn Company in 1886 with his invention of the friable pill.

Our routine was always to go to the pharmacy first, where our father, one of the senior executives at Upjohn, would usually ask one of the pharmacists to put a leech or two on each of our forearms. We tolerated this exercise yet were grateful that few therapeutic practices still called for the use of leeches.

Some 50 years later, well after The Upjohn Company had closed its operations on Disneyland's Main Street, U.S.A., I was excited to learn that the University of Arizona College of Pharmacy had taken possession of the former pharmacy's displays and intended to use them in a new exhibit in its history museum. When the museum's curator, Stephen Hall, contacted me, I was very pleased to hear his enthusiastic aspirations for the exhibit. I imagined the Disneyland displays as part of a broader exhibit on the history of pharmacy, which would include a history beginning with roots, berries, bark—and yes, leeches—running into the vastness of molecular biology and all that we still need to learn about human health.

That phone conversation convinced me that the industry's many scientific and medical discoveries would be presented in a fair, accurate, and meaningful manner. I never anticipated the depth in which the curator would describe the significance of the industry and the remarkable story of the many intersections of the Disney and Upjohn families.

I have not yet seen the new exhibits at the University of Arizona's pharmacy museum, but a trusted colleague who recently toured the museum confirms that Stephen's work is successful in blending artifacts, including many pieces from the Upjohn Pharmacy at Disneyland, with an effective use of technology to present the centuries-old history of pharmaceuticals through the present day in an elegant, accessible, and entertaining manner. He also reports that the exhibit provides an insightful view of the evolution of the U.S. pharmaceutical industry and its important role in improving global health.

Stephen's gift for seeing points of intersection where others saw none makes this book most enjoyable. His account of Walt Disney's childhood in Kansas City and the most certain exposure to The Upjohn Company's Kansas City office showcases Stephen's skillful assessment of historical places and events. Yet to me what stands out most prominently is the recognition of a coincidental use of sugar by the inventive patriarchs of both families. Dr. Upjohn was able to use sugar in his friable pill to forever change medicinal chemistry, while Walt Disney and Julie Andrews gave voice to Pamela Lyndon Travers' character Mary Poppins and her iconic command that "a spoonful of sugar helps the medicine go down." Stephen draws from both to give title to his most delightful book.

Donald R. Parfet retired in 2000 from The Upjohn Company's successor company, Pharmacia, where he was the last direct descendant of Dr. Upjohn to have been employed. In 2003, Pfizer acquired Pharmacia.

— Donald R. Parfet

Leeches are not this cute.

The Upjohn Pharmacy at night. To the left is Main Street, U.S.A., and to the right is Center Street. A large mortar-and-pestle-shaped lamp hangs on the corner of the building. © Coit Museum of Pharmacy & Health Sciences, The University of Arizona College of Pharmacy (used with permission)

Preface

My connection to the Upjohn Pharmacy in Disneyland began in 2012, 42 years after it closed. As I started my first year of graduate school, starry-eyed and anxious to become a curator at the Louvre, I set out to find a museum where I could gain volunteer experience. After every other museum in Tucson, Arizona, rejected me (seriously, who turns down free labor?), the curator of the History of Pharmacy Museum—a place neither I nor anyone I knew had ever heard of—took a chance on me.

Though the pharmacy museum had been open for almost 50 years, it had never had a full-time curator (or even a staff member, for that matter), nor had it had any sort of recordkeeping, save for some handwritten notes from the 1960s that bore no modern relevance. Since its inception, the museum had always been a one-man labor of love, a sort of glorified side project for the three volunteer historians who had overseen it at different times throughout the years. People who had lived in Tucson for decades had never heard of the museum—in part because it never did any kind of advertising—and the museum's ramshackle displays were woefully overdue for an update. (I still shudder at the thought of the hideous pink fabric that lined some of the exhibits from the 1980s.)

For half a century, my predecessors had collected and collected—anything and everything—resulting in a world-class but nightmarishly disorganized assortment of artifacts in overflowing storage. No one knew what was in the collection, how much there was, when it had been acquired, or where any of it had come from. When I started working at the museum, it was completely normal for me to come across unknown boxes with labels like "ASSORTED POISONS" or "ACID."

The curator at that time, Dick Wiedhopf, was one of the assistant deans of the University of Arizona College of Pharmacy, which houses the museum. Though he was a historian by avocation, Dick rarely had time to devote to the museum because his constant stream of administrative responsibilities always had to take precedence. This meant that, through no fault of his own, the museum was usually near the bottom of his priority list.

Several years before I began volunteering, the museum had received the artifact collection from the Upjohn Pharmacy in Disneyland, but like much of the rest of the museum's inventory, this collection had remained in storage, boxes unopened, ever since. On my very first day of volunteering, Dick showed me the museum's storage room (well, one of them anyway), where a mountain of boxes sat piled high. When he told me they were from Disneyland, I was immediately intrigued. Dick had no idea what was inside the boxes, and I knew nothing at all about pharmacy or its history, but the simple mention of Disneyland roped me in.

My first task was to unpack all 900-some items so that we could see what we had. I will never forget Dick's jovial, mustached smile as he looked at me, a 22-year-old kid clutching a skateboard, handed me the key to a storage room containing a priceless collection of antiques, and said, "Have fun!" It took me several days just to unpack everything, but each box felt like a treasure chest, full of mystery and excitement.

Some of the items were in rough shape. The hundred-plus apothecary vessels had had masking tape applied to them to keep their lids and stoppers in place, but after years in storage in the dry Arizona climate, they were covered in stubborn globs of sticky residue and petrified tape. Dick brought me a kitchen sponge and a bottle of Goo Gone to clean them with, a project that took me two weeks and taught me what carpal tunnel syndrome is.

I continued volunteering at the museum throughout graduate school, and as I neared the end of my studies, Dick gave in to my constant badgering and offered me a full-time job. (Did I mention he controlled the budget?)

Narrowly escaping the likely unemployment of a library science degree, I became the museum's first assistant curator in 2014, and later took over as curator after Dick retired. I was the first person to hold a full-time position at the History of Pharmacy Museum, and the first to give its magnificent collection the focused attention it so desperately needed.

Since the day I began unpacking those boxes of apothecary curios, the Upjohn Pharmacy has held a special place in my heart. What began as merely a means to gain volunteer experience turned into my first professional job, a job that presented me with amazing, once-in-a-lifetime opportunities. This book is a passion project, years in the making, and it is now my privilege to share the story of the Upjohn Pharmacy with the world.

— Stephen Hall, MA

A hanging show globe adorns a window of the Upjohn Pharmacy.
© Coit Museum of Pharmacy & Health Sciences,
The University of Arizona College of Pharmacy (used with permission)

Introduction

"To all who come to this happy place: welcome. Disneyland is your land. Here age relives fond memories of the past... and here youth may savor the challenge and promise of the future."

With these words on July 17, 1955, Walt Disney unveiled his grandest achievement. As the teeming crowd, thousands in number, poured into Disneyland on opening day, one of the first sights they saw was a Victorian-style apothecary shop. Situated on the corner of Main and Center streets, partway between the park entrance and Sleeping Beauty Castle, the little shop invited visitors to step back in time.

As decorative show globes, a classic symbol of the pharmacy profession, glistened in the summer-sunlit windows, a pair of friendly young pharmacists in 1890s period garb worked at the counter. Children and their parents marveled at a jar of live leeches and gazed through two-centuries-old microscopes. Under the warm light of colorful, 19th-century German pendant lamps, guests admired the plethora of antique apothecary wares.

This was the Upjohn Pharmacy.

Fred Ekstein, one of the two licensed pharmacists who worked in the store, said of opening day, "It was hectic and hotter than all get-out. The guests were pretty good, and I think they enjoyed themselves."

His colleague, pharmacist Phil Harvey, recalled, "Opening day was both wonderful and filled with chaos. People were everywhere. It was a great place—there was nothing else like it in the world."

The exterior of the Upjohn Pharmacy, facing Main Street, U.S.A.
© Coit Museum of Pharmacy & Health Sciences, The University of Arizona College of Pharmacy (used with permission)

℞

Background

"Credit for store development goes to a number of people. Ad manager [Jack] Gauntlett first saw its possibilities as a vehicle for the Upjohn institutional message." (*Overflow*, September 1955, pg. 333)

The story of the Upjohn Pharmacy is one of good fortune, a story of all the right people working together to create something truly special.

The Upjohn Pharmacy grew out of a friendship between Walt Disney and Donald Gilmore, the managing director and board chairman of The Upjohn Company. From 1886 until 1995, The Upjohn Company was a giant in the pharmaceutical industry, headquartered in Kalamazoo, Michigan, and well-known for making drug products like Cheracol and Kaopectate.

Donald Gilmore's primary residence was in Michigan, but he owned a second home at the Smoke Tree Ranch, a high-end community in Palm Springs, California. This home, located near the home of Walt and Lillian Disney, provided Gilmore and his wife, Genevieve, an escape from the frigid Michigan winters.[1]

As part-time neighbors and full-time friends, Gilmore and Disney had a strong relationship. During the winter months, the two men were lawn bowling partners. The rest of the year, they kept in touch by writing each other letters. Disney made multiple trips to Kalamazoo to see Gilmore, and even sold him, for the cost of shipping to Michigan, a 1930 Rolls-Royce and matching set piece[2] that were used in Disney's film *The Gnome-Mobile*. Gilmore was an avid car collector, and he went on to establish the Gilmore Car Museum, where this vehicle is still on display today.[3] Though he was neither a medical doctor nor a pharmacist, Donald Gilmore had close ties to the health sciences: he was both the son-in-law and stepson of W. E. Upjohn, the founder of The Upjohn Company.

The initial idea for the Upjohn Pharmacy was the brainchild of the company's advertising director, Jack Gauntlett.[4] "I thought that [it] would be a wonderful gimmick," he said. "I was trying to do things that would reach the public instead of just doctors and druggists." When he approached Gilmore with the idea, Gilmore loved it. "Anybody else would say that this was goofy and to forget it, but he was immediately interested," Gauntlett recalled years later. "What I hadn't known was that Don knew Walt Disney."[5]

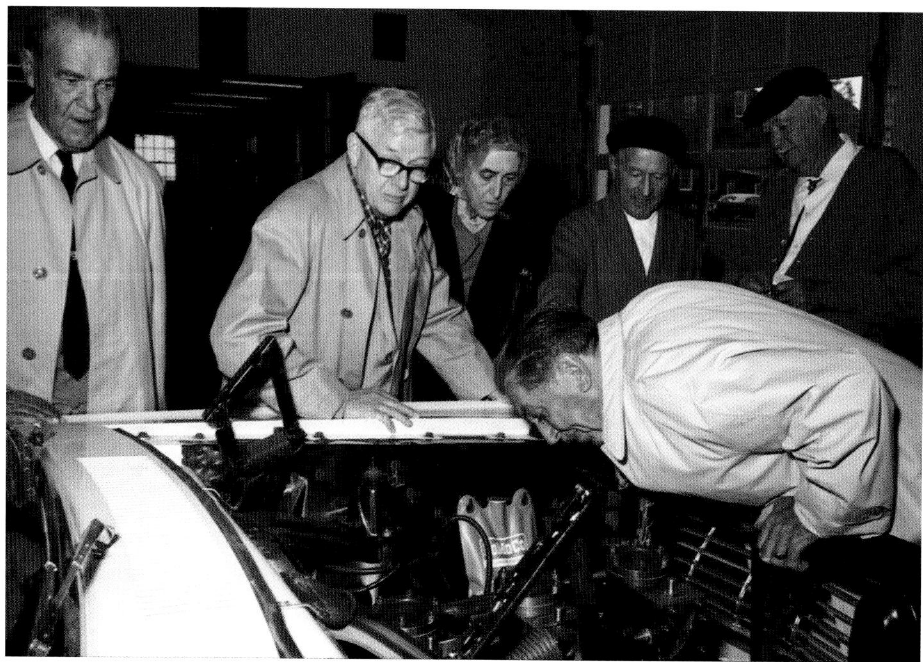

Top Left: Donald Gilmore (left) greets Walt Disney at the Kalamazoo Airport upon Disney's arrival in West Michigan.

Bottom Left: Walt Disney greets Genevieve Gilmore upon arriving in West Michigan.

Top Right: Walt Disney drives a Stanley Steamer, as Donald Gilmore rides in the backseat.

Bottom Right: Walt Disney, Donald Gilmore, and others examine a car engine.
All images © Gilmore Car Museum (used with permission)

Arm in arm, Donald Gilmore and Walt Disney strike a pose as Disney holds Gilmore's hat. © Gilmore Car Museum (used with permission)

Walt Disney plays with a dog at the Gilmore family cottage at Gull Lake. © Gilmore Car Museum (used with permission)

Walt Disney enjoys coffee with Donald Gilmore (left) and others at Gilmore's cottage at Gull Lake. © Gilmore Car Museum (used with permission)

Walt Disney and Donald Gilmore converse in the Upjohn hangar at the Kalamazoo Airport. © Gilmore Car Museum (used with permission)

Top Left: The Gilmore Car Museum today. © Stephen Hall

Bottom Left: The 1930 Rolls-Royce used in Disney's The Gnome-Mobile, on display at the Gilmore Car Museum. © Stephen Hall

Top Right: At the Gilmore Car Museum, author Stephen Hall sits on the oversized backseat set piece from The Gnome-Mobile. © Stephen Hall

In an interview with the author, a former Upjohn pilot named Virgil Williams shared his memories of Jack Gauntlett and the Gilmores. About Gauntlett he said:

> Jack, besides being a passenger, was a good friend of mine. He and I played golf together several times, and we flew him quite a lot. Jack was a wonderful person. He was so common. I remember flying him—I'd go in the back and talk to him—we'd talk about golf, hunting, whatever. He was just a happy person.

And about the Gilmores he said:

> They were wonderful people. Donald was very interesting to talk to. He and Genevieve were both very down-to-earth people. They always provided us lunch, and the lunch was always watercress sandwiches. We all used to laugh about Mrs. Gilmore's watercress sandwiches—she made them and brought them on board."[6]

In the years leading up to Disneyland's grand opening, Walt Disney invited numerous companies to have a presence in the park, including PepsiCo, Richfield Oil, and General Electric. Bank of America had put up $17 million to finance the park's construction, but this had proved insufficient to cover the total cost. In need of extra funding, Disney mortgaged his Palm Springs home, cashed in his life insurance, and sought corporate sponsorships.

At this point, all the pieces were in place. With Gauntlett's unique advertising vision, Gilmore's enthusiasm for his idea, and an existing connection to Walt Disney, who was currently looking for outside investors, The Upjohn Company signed on to sponsor a pharmacy in Disneyland.[7]

A page from the Gilmore Car Museum's guest book, featuring an entry from Walt Disney. © Stephen Hall

Development

"The building's design is the direct result of research and work poured into it by our own people as well as the designers and architects in the Disneyland organization." (*Overflow*, June 1955, pg. 183)

The first step in developing the Upjohn Pharmacy was to conduct historical research. To do this, Jack Gauntlett traveled to New York City to visit real, working apothecaries that had been in operation for many years. Photographs from the June 1955 issue of *The Overflow*, Upjohn's sales magazine, suggest that Gauntlett visited, specifically, the apothecaries of J. Leon Lascoff & Son, Wm. M. Olliffe, and H. A. Cassebeer.[8] In order to get a wholistic picture of what these stores were like, Gauntlett studied their architecture, their interior design, and their overall ambience.[9]

Once Gauntlett's initial research was complete, Dr. A. Garrard MacLeod, a physician, antique enthusiast, and the editor of Upjohn's scientific publication, *Scope* magazine, spent five weeks traveling the country in search of authentic, period-appropriate pieces to use in the store. Starting his hunt locally, MacLeod attended an auction of medical antiques at a home in Kalamazoo.[10] He acquired the first items there, then expanded

APOTHECARIES
LASCOFF & SON
ANALYSES PRESCRIPTIONS CHEMICALS
Otto Mach
FUR STORAGE

Page 19: Interior of the apothecary shop of H. A. Cassebeer (established 1843), one of the inspirations for the Upjohn Pharmacy. © Coit Museum of Pharmacy & Health Sciences, The University of Arizona College of Pharmacy (used with permission)

Page 20: Exterior of the apothecary shop of J. Leon Lascoff & Son (established 1899), one of the inspirations for the Upjohn Pharmacy. © Coit Museum of Pharmacy & Health Sciences, The University of Arizona College of Pharmacy (used with permission)

This page, left: Exterior of the apothecary shop of Wm. M. Olliffe (established 1805), one of the inspirations for the Upjohn Pharmacy. © Coit Museum of Pharmacy & Health Sciences, The University of Arizona College of Pharmacy (used with permission)

This page, above: Interior of one of the apothecary shops that served as inspiration for the Upjohn Pharmacy. The Upjohn store featured numerous apothecary vessels like these, as well as near-identical pendant lamps. © Coit Museum of Pharmacy & Health Sciences, The University of Arizona College of Pharmacy (used with permission)

his search to include doctors' offices, antique stores, and private collections around the United States. *Overflow* noted in November 1955 that major finds were made in Michigan, Illinois, Louisiana, South Carolina, Pennsylvania, New York, and New Jersey. In total, over 1,000 pieces were displayed in the Upjohn Pharmacy, many of them collected by Dr. MacLeod.

Renowned designer Will Burtin had been working with The Upjohn Company for more than a decade by the time the Disneyland project began, and his efforts had transformed the company's public image. In light of pharmacy's rapid advancements following World War II, Burtin's sleek aesthetics represented a new age of innovation for Upjohn.[11] Among his other work at the company, Burtin was the art editor of *Scope*, and he was put in charge of the Upjohn Pharmacy's design.[12] Coincidentally, Burtin's wife, Hilda, had had a previous association with Disney—in prewar Germany, she drew animation cells of Pluto for the company.

In an interview with the author, MacLeod's son George recalled the meticulous effort applied to the Upjohn Pharmacy's design:

> Especially that year before it opened, [Garrard] and Will were there all the time. Disney wanted to have control over the design of the pharmacy because it was his thing. Their designers came up

Apothecary vessels from the Upjohn Pharmacy (promotional photograph). © Coit Museum of Pharmacy & Health Sciences, The University of Arizona College of Pharmacy (used with permission)

> with an idea, they showed to Will [and Garrard], and it was not a good representation of a late-1800s pharmacy.
>
> So Will and [Garrard] said, "We can't accept that. We're not going to be here if that's what it's going to look like." They said, "Well, do you have a better idea?" And they did. They came up with a design of their own, and that's how it ended up.

In a fusion of old and new, Burtin's design included two sections. The larger, main area was a replica apothecary, and a smaller, back room housed a contemporary exhibit that showcased modern-day Upjohn.

The pharmacy was designed with five entrances, such that it was accessible from all directions. The Upjohn team admitted that it had taken some creative liberties, deviating from authentic store design to assure a manageable traffic pattern. After all, its desirable location within Disneyland, en route to the inevitable destinations, meant that visitors were constantly coming and going.

On April 8, 1955, just 100 days before the park opened for preview, Upjohn's lease agreement was finalized. The agreement gave Upjohn 45 days to submit its plans and noted that, if Disney did not approve them, revised plans would have to be submitted within 30 days thereafter. It is unclear exactly how long it took Upjohn to receive final approval, but if the company had used the entire time frame allotted, including submitting revised plans, there would have been less than four weeks left for fabrication and installation!

Jack Gauntlett (left) and Will Burtin (right) work on a model of the Upjohn Pharmacy.
© The Upjohn Company (used under fair use)

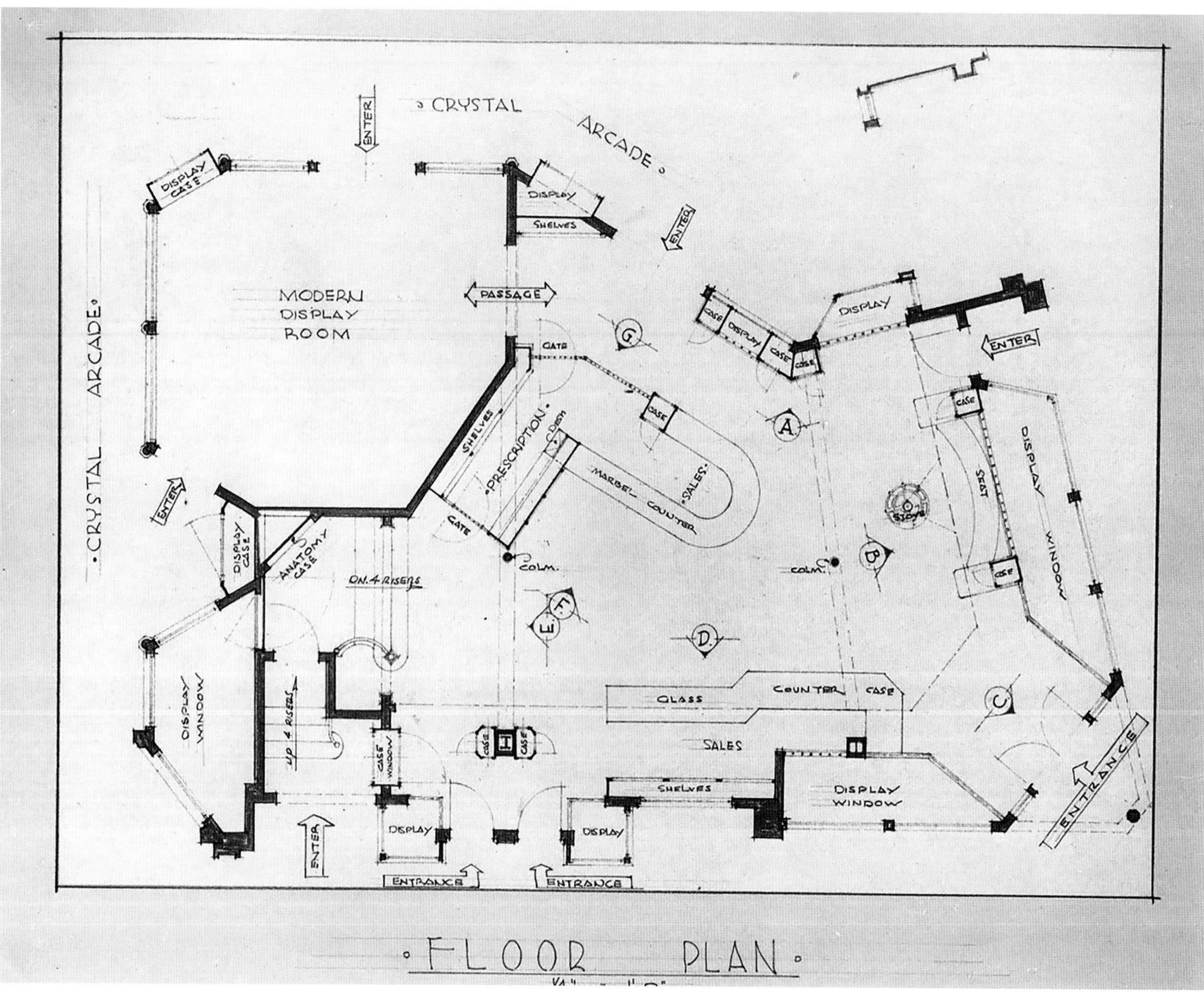

Will Burtin's floor plan for the Upjohn Pharmacy. © The Upjohn Company (used under fair use)

(Left to right) Walt Disney, Jack Gauntlett, and Donald Gilmore present a concept sketch of the Upjohn Pharmacy. *© The Upjohn Company (used under fair use)*

Construction/Opening

"There has been some disagreement on the architectural authenticity of the pharmacy itself, but no one disagrees on the authenticity and atmosphere of the reality created by the more than 1,000 items dragged from attics, antique shops, doctors' offices and shop windows by Dr. Garrard MacLeod, Scope editor, and designer Will Burtin." (*Overflow*, November 1955, pg. 402)

As the Upjohn Pharmacy was being built, advertising director Jack Gauntlett traveled to California 12 times to oversee its construction. "It was one of the hardest jobs I ever did," he said. "Everything had to be built [from scratch]." Gauntlett had to comply with Disney's own specifications, as well. For example, there were to be no square corners, unless absolutely necessary.

Construction of the Upjohn Pharmacy took longer than expected. Years later, in-store pharmacist Phil Harvey said, "I think they were still pounding nails in our facility up until the time we were scheduled to open." In actuality, Harvey's memory was correct; construction was going on past midnight on the night of July 16, 1955, just hours before Disneyland opened for preview.

The following morning, the building was in launchable shape, but much of the work remained undone. The pharmacy's iconic mortar-and-pestle-shaped lamp would not be installed for at least a few weeks, and its interior took even longer to complete. The September 1955 issue of *Overflow* stated, "Because the park was pandemonium, the exhibits unfinished, and the interior of the drugstore incomplete, no inside photos were taken. The jars and bottles are now being filled with crude drugs, and the drugstore should be truly complete this month."

Despite a shaky start, an official, if modest dedication ceremony took place on July 18, 1955, the day Disneyland officially opened to the public. There were two ribbon-cuttings, one by Upjohn's sales director, Fred Allen, and the other by representatives from two California pharmacy associations and the publisher of *West Coast Druggist* magazine.

Due to scheduling conflicts, neither Donald Gilmore nor president E. G. Upjohn were able to attend the opening. Two weeks earlier, a representative from Disney had invited both men to a cocktail reception at Slue Foot Sue's Golden Horseshoe on the night of the 16th, but Dr. Upjohn replied that Gilmore was in Europe, and he himself had "a commitment in Florida on that day which can't very well be broken." Fred Allen and Jack Gauntlett went in their stead. Additionally, 80 park tickets were given out to West Coast Upjohn employees and their families.

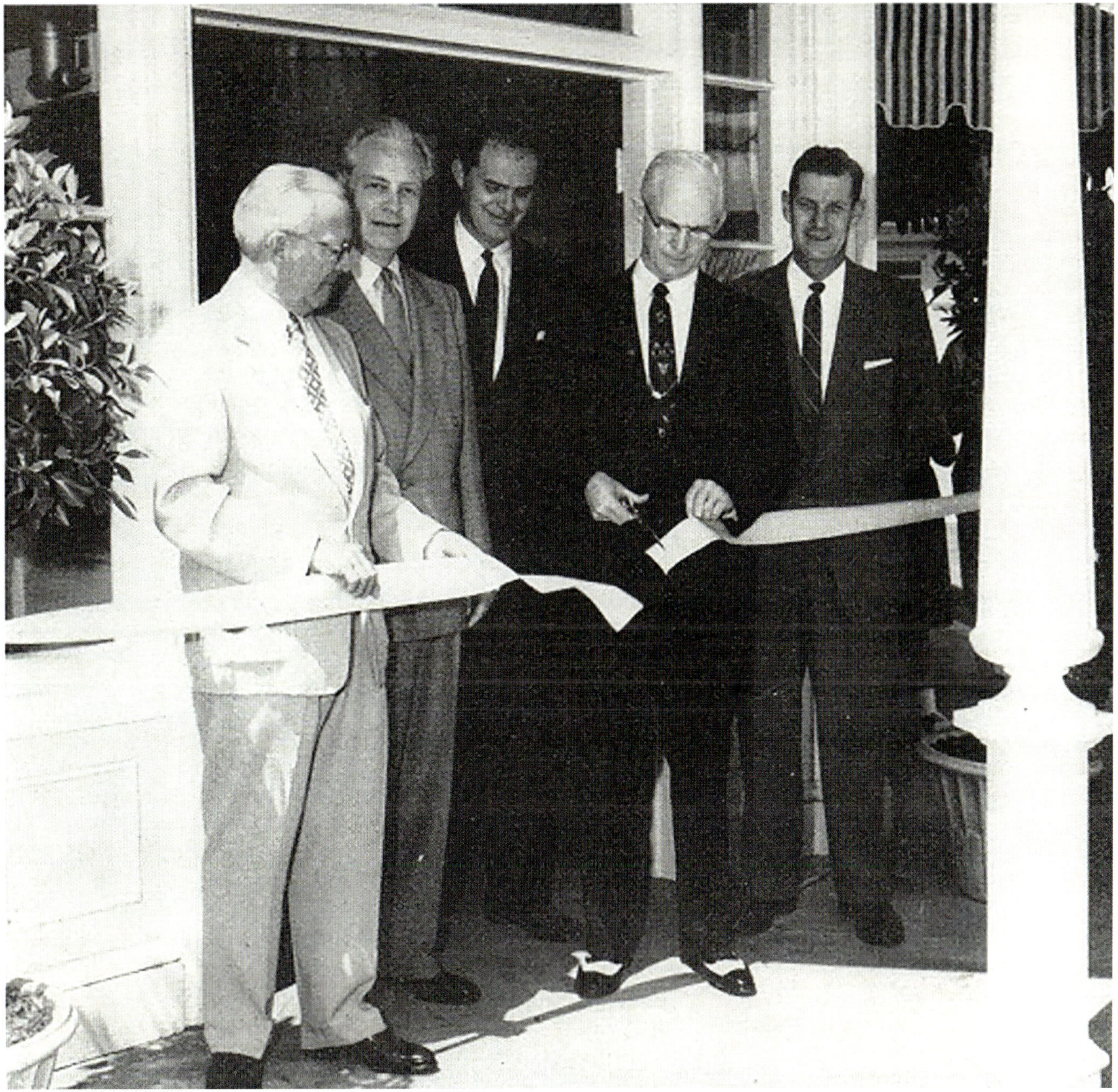

(Left to right) Store Manager Leo Austin,
Los Angeles Office Manager Lyman Williams,
Advertising Director Jack Gauntlett,
Sales Director Fred Allen, and
Los Angeles Sales Manager Karl Zorn
at the dedication ceremony of the Upjohn Pharmacy.

Marketing

"Our only reason for sponsoring the store is that its presence in Disneyland constitutes sound, inexpensive, advertising with exciting possibilities. As Disney reaps the profits of his latest work, Upjohn will get full advertising value." (*Overflow*, April 1955, pg. 117)

Overflow's first announcement of the Upjohn Pharmacy put it succinctly: "In short, Upjohn is in Disneyland because it gives us a new effective form of institutional advertising." With an upfront cost of only $29,600, Upjohn saw the incredible marketing potential its Disneyland store presented.

Early estimates predicted that six million people would visit Disneyland annually, many of whom would be adults visiting from out of state.[13] In the months leading up to the park's grand opening, Upjohn worked overtime to push the message of its shop throughout the country. Leo Austin, a former sales manager for Upjohn's Los Angeles branch, had been called out of retirement to manage the store. He took on the task of West Coast public relations, while Jack Gauntlett oversaw the rest of the country.

Their goal was to generate public interest and to assure America's druggists that the Upjohn Pharmacy would serve "to point up the role of the drugstore proprietor." To prevent any misunderstandings, the company wanted to make it clear that it was not entering into the retail pharmacy world and that its pretend store in Disneyland would be a service, rather than a competitor, to real drugstores everywhere.

Naturally, the store itself was full of company-branded materials, primarily in the contemporary exhibit space. In addition to this self-promotion, another valuable facet of the Upjohn Pharmacy's branding was its four-person in-store staff: pharmacists Phil Harvey and Fred Ekstein, and clerks Betty Lou Foley and Juanita Eloise Goodwin.

Phil Harvey described the staff's role, saying:

> Our function, basically, was public relations and advertising for the company. We would be there to answer any questions people would have about our products or the antiques on display. But we also handed out PAC [aspirin] tablets and little square bottles of Unicap vitamins[14] as a means of promoting Upjohn... It was good advertising.

A sample bottle of Unicap vitamins from the Upjohn Pharmacy. © Stephen Hall

Harvey and Ekstein both hailed from Long Beach, California, and they came to the Upjohn Pharmacy after working in retail drugstores. Ekstein had been employed at Sav-On Drugs in Long Beach, and Harvey had co-owned a drugstore in Torrance. Foley and Goodwin, though not pharmacists themselves (female pharmacists were few in number at the time), both had connections to the profession. Foley's husband, Basil, was an Upjohn sales representative in Los Angeles, and Goodwin had previous experience as a pharmacy clerk.

The Upjohn Pharmacy opened during a veritable renaissance of drug marketing. Between 1939 and 1959, U.S. drug sales had grown from $300 million to $2.3 billion annually, the primary catalyst being the advent of prescription medications. As these became commonplace, drug companies altered their marketing strategies. Believing that patients were unable to make informed medical decisions on their own, companies largely stopped advertising to consumers and instead aimed their promotions directly at health professionals.

Estimates from 1958 posited that the drug industry had by that time printed more than 3.7 billion pages of advertisements in medical journals, sent over 740 million pieces of marketing mail, and made up to 20 million phone calls to pharmacists and physicians. In light of their prescribing powers, physicians received the brunt of this messaging; about 90 percent of it was directed at them, the other 10 percent at pharmacists and hospitals.

This represented a complete paradigm shift from the beginning of the century and made the Upjohn Pharmacy—situated in one of the most public forums in the world and aimed squarely at the general public—seem all the more unique.

A key part of this shift toward provider-specific advertising was the introduction of sales representatives known as "detail men."[15] Author Jeremy Greene notes that this term came from these salesmen's performance, half sales pitch and half educational service, through which they presented doctors with the prescribing information, or "details," about new products. In an age where new drugs were constantly coming to market, physicians rarely had the bandwidth to keep up with them all. Thus, detail men acted as liaisons, offering personalized service and providing elevator speeches with pertinent product information.

To help incentivize providers to buy from their company's catalog, detail men would often pass out promotional items. Some were as simple as branded trinkets given to graduates of pharmacy programs. Others were ongoing series of collectibles that encouraged practitioners to continue supporting the companies that made them. Still others were reproductions of antique apothecary wares or prints of exquisite oil paintings.[16]

At the end of the 1920s, there were about 2,000 detail men in the United States, but within 30 years, this figure had grown to more than 15,000. Simply put, the new classes of drugs on the market necessitated creative, dynamic forms of advertising. (The Upjohn Pharmacy itself may be the most prescient example of this!)

A textbook from 1949 outlines the desirable characteristics of a detail man. Arthur Peterson's *Pharmaceutical Selling, "Detailing," and Sales Training* notes that detail men should have, among other qualities:

- Good appearance
- A pleasing personality
- A good speaking voice and effective delivery
- A suitable educational background
- Good retail experience

These traits undoubtedly aligned with those that Disney would have wanted for its park staff. Drug companies also particularly sought licensed pharmacists for detail roles because their educational background allowed them to speak the language of the physicians to whom they marketed. Given Harvey's and Ekstein's education, their professional licensure, and their role advertising Upjohn and its products, they essentially acted as public-facing detail men for The Upjohn Company.

Notes Jeremy Greene, "Conscious efforts were made to mold the detail man's appearance into something that marketing managers saw as emblematic of their strategic goals." While this usually meant dressing the salesman in a well-tailored suit with a hat and tie to match, in the case of Disneyland and the Upjohn Pharmacy, it meant dressing the staff in proper, turn-of-the-century attire. Though this may have made them look different than other detail men of the day, it played to both Disney's and Upjohn's strategic goal: advertising, through a rose-colored look at the past.

Additionally, it should be noted that the Upjohn Pharmacy did indeed have special marketing strategies specifically for pharmacists and physicians. As the *Disneyland Line* noted in a retrospective:

> One of the services The Upjohn Company provided was to take Polaroid pictures when physicians or fellow druggists and their families would stop by. A special photo holder, which bore the Disneyland and Upjohn logos, served not only as a souvenir, but also a subtle reminder of both Disneyland and Upjohn.

Pharmacist Phil Harvey working at the Upjohn Pharmacy's prescription counter in full period garb. Behind him is the store's backsplash, adorned with apothecary wares, a French balance, and a Wedgwood bust of Hippocrates. Above him hangs the large Upjohn clock and three of the 12 leaded-glass pendant lamps. © The Upjohn Company (used under fair use)

Polaroid photo holder from the Upjohn Pharmacy (front). © The Upjohn Company (used under fair use)

Polaroid photo holder from the Upjohn Pharmacy (inside). © The Upjohn Company (used under fair use)

IT WAS A GENUINE PLEASURE to have you visit The Upjohn Pharmacy in Disneyland and to share with you the rich traditions of medicine and pharmacy.

Since the 1880's, remarkable progress has been made in medicine and pharmacy. The Upjohn Company is proud of the contributions it has made through unending research to develop new medicines and through the expansion of facilities to make these discoveries widely available. Most of all, we are proud of the way more than six thousand employees are still adhering to the mandate laid down in 1886 by Dr. W. E. Upjohn, founder of The Upjohn Company:

"Keep the Quality Up."

This targeted advertising practice was comparable to traditional detail men passing out branded knickknacks to doctors and druggists. Of course, it was exactly this type of direct-to-provider promotion that caused great scrutiny and concern over ethics, even being referred to as a "corporate medicine show." For this reason, in 1959, drug marketing became a topic of congressional hearings. Author Nancy Tomes writes that, when faced with criticism:

> The ethical companies repeatedly tried to reassure the profession that their marketing and advertising policies would always adhere to the high road of life-saving education. Yet, perhaps inevitably, observers both within and outside medicine began to worry about the negative impact of the new-style drug promotions on physicians' prescribing habits and the doctor-patient relationship.

By incorporating real, recognizable products into its re-creation

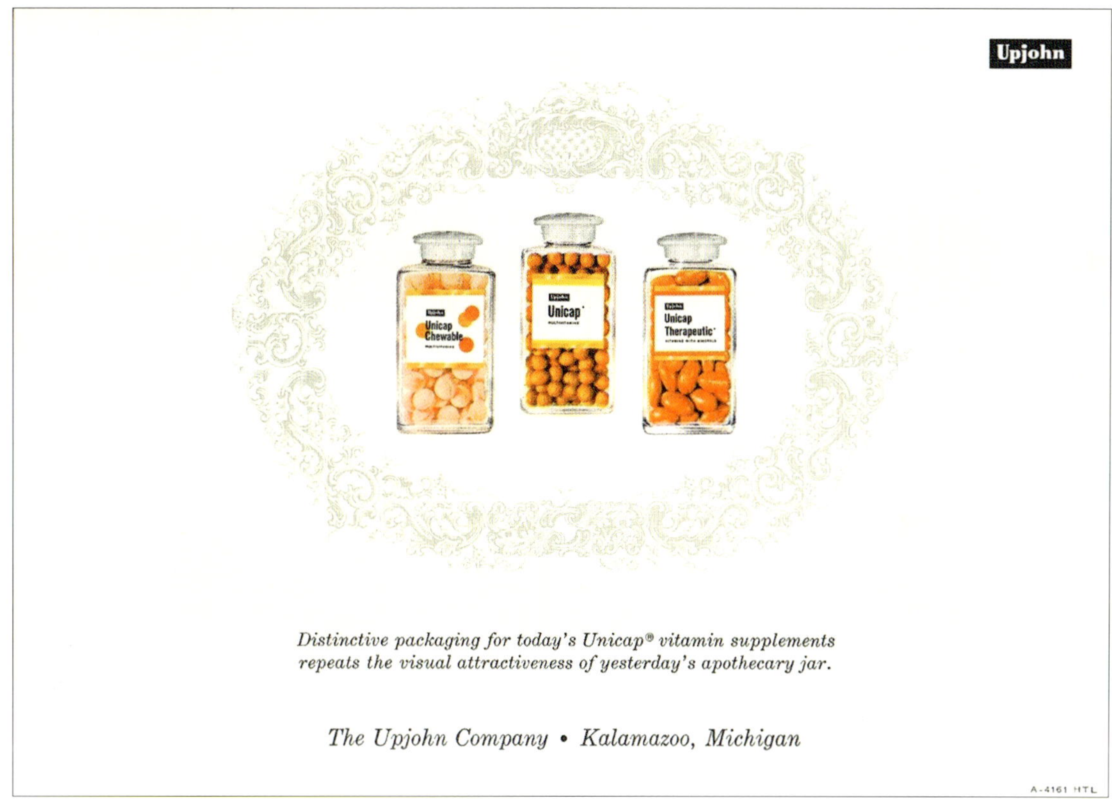

Polaroid photo holder from the Upjohn Pharmacy (back). *© The Upjohn Company (used under fair use)*

of history, The Upjohn Company established a sense of realism in the store for its visitors, a mixture of brand promotion and nostalgic whimsy. The pharmacy was not, of course, an actual retail drugstore, but rather a museum of sorts, and a life-sized advertisement for the company. Patrons would come away with a souvenir booklet about Upjohn, a specially marked vitamin bottle, and up to four different promotional postcards, all items to remind them of their visit and to help them to mentally connect Upjohn to quality healthcare.

During the planning process, The Upjohn Company had discussed the possibility of selling certain drug products—its lease agreement allowed for it—but the company ultimately decided not to.[17] Gauntlett recalled, "Finally, because so many people would come in and ask, 'Do you have any Citrocarbonate or Kaopectate?' we made these products available in the Disney Medical Clinic for treating people who had accidents. Then we would say, 'Just go there and get some.'"

Experience

"The Upjohn Pharmacy is both something new and ancient—new to this generation of Americans accustomed to the sight of gay colors, streamlined design, shiny chrome, but familiar to those who still remember the apothecary of our forefathers." (Excerpt from the Upjohn Pharmacy's informational pamphlet)

Visitors to the Upjohn Pharmacy were immersed in a meticulously detailed view of history. The colorful glow of a 19th-century mortar-and-pestle-shaped lamp illuminated the entrance and at night projected the ℞ symbol onto the sidewalk below.[18] As if stepping through a portal, visitors to the pharmacy were transported to a bygone age.

The mahogany fixtures in the main store area were all faithful re-creations of Victorian apothecary furniture, built by master craftsmen and complete with marble slab countertops. Thanks to the tireless work of Garrard MacLeod and Will Burtin, the cabinetry was adorned with genuine items that would have been considered essential to a pharmacy of that day.

Among these thousand-some pieces were two enormous majolica vats for olive oil[19] and four large, reverse-painted glass

Previous page: The Upjohn Pharmacy's iconic mortar-and-pestle lamp in daylight. © Coit Museum of Pharmacy & Health Sciences, The University of Arizona College of Pharmacy (used with permission)

Right: Pharmacist Phil Harvey compounds behind the prescription counter. © The Upjohn Company (used under fair use)

vessels with glimmering gold leaf and detailed cartouches of magnesia, Iceland moss, larkspur, and foxglove. An impressive wooden clock, bearing a three-dimensional relief of the original Upjohn logo hung near the ceiling, illuminated by a dozen leaded-glass pendant lamps.[20]

At the prescription counter, druggists Harvey and Ekstein, in era-appropriate costumes, compounded as guests looked on, using mortars and pestles as old as 1575. Behind them, an ornate backsplash boasted a portion of the more than 250 apothecary jars and bottles that lined the store. In the center of this display stood a massive French balance from 1840, positioned below a Wedgwood bust of Hippocrates, circa 1800. Showcases displayed drugs, cosmetics, and medical equipment, many in their original packaging, which had come from Morgan's Pharmacy in Philadelphia.

Left: Guests examine drug and cosmetic products displayed in showcases at the Upjohn Pharmacy, 1959.

Right: A young guest tries her hand at using a mortar and pestle, 1960. Both images from the collection of davelandweb.com (used with permission)

THE UPJOHN COMPANY
EUROPEAN ME
LEECHES
BRED ON THE FAMOUS HIRUDORIUM
LEECH FARMS IN EUROPE

Left: A patron examines the Upjohn Pharmacy's famous leech jar, 1960.

Above: The "Dapper Dans" perform in the Upjohn Pharmacy.
Both images from the collection of davelandweb.com (used with permission)

Nearby, a jar of live leeches from the Hirudorium Leech Farms in Europe attracted the eyes (and perhaps churned the stomachs) of inquiring visitors. Along the walls were turn-of-the-century advertisements from real pharmacies, such as McGuire's in Petaluma, California. The north side of the building offered seating around a potbellied stove, from which patrons could admire antique medical equipment as they pretended to wait for their prescriptions to be filled. Among the most remarkable pieces was a wood and paper microscope, made in 1700 and still in working order.

The authenticity was not limited to the visual. An article in *The Louisiana Pharmacist* said:

> To anyone who has ever been in an old-fashioned pharmacy, perhaps the most vivid memory was the host of strange, exotic—and wonderful—smells that permeated it. Among the items stocked in [the Upjohn Pharmacy's] apothecary jars and show globes are vanilla beans, elm bark, whole select sassafras bark, decorticated cardamom seed, sesame seed, licorice root sticks, lavendar [*sic*] flowers, fennel seed... cloves, sandalwood, rosemary leaves, whole nutmeg, Ceylon cinnamon quills and Jamaica ginger.

These aromatic herbs were regularly ground through a 75-year-old herb grinder to make the store smell authentic. Upjohn had also worked with retailers of old-fashioned sweets to display their products in countertop candy jars, to be distributed to children.

Media outlets praised the store's design and extraordinary attention to detail. *Drug Topics* said, "Everything in the Upjohn Pharmacy is in harmony with the early century setting," even down to the dormer and arch-top windows in the second story. The *Disneylander* magazine referred to it as "one of the most elaborate museums of authentic pharmaceutical wares, furnishings and equipment in existence." Still another outlet called it "a symbol of progress" and "a tribute to the importance of the contribution made to better health by the nation's pharmacists."

One of the Upjohn Pharmacy's window displays. © Coit Museum of Pharmacy & Health Sciences, The University of Arizona College of Pharmacy (used with permission)

Upper left: White, painted-glass vessels, labeled for magnesia and Iceland moss (promotional photograph). © Coit Museum of Pharmacy & Health Sciences, The University of Arizona College of Pharmacy (used with permission)

Lower left: Blue, painted-glass vessels, with details of larkspur and foxglove (promotional photograph). © Coit Museum of Pharmacy & Health Sciences, The University of Arizona College of Pharmacy (used with permission)

Below: Exterior of the Upjohn Pharmacy, August 1962. On display in the bay windows next to the Crystal Arcade are the large majolica olive oil vats. From the collection of Disney History 101 (used with permission).

Left: Interior of the Upjohn Pharmacy, showing countertop candy jars and a large, pear-shaped carboy, 1960.

Below: Interior of the Upjohn Pharmacy, looking out toward the Carnation ice cream parlor, 1957.

Right: Apothecary vessels on display, including candy jars, lion-shaped candle holders, and a seated show globe, 1956. All three images from the collection of davelandweb.com (used with permission).

Left: Apothecary glassware on display in the Upjohn Pharmacy, 1956. From the collection of davelandweb.com (used with permission).

Below: The interior of the Upjohn Pharmacy's contemporary exhibit, showing the company's production timeline in four rotating columns. To the right is the large transparency of the Portage Road plant near Kalamazoo, Michigan. The doorway to the larger apothecary exhibit is visible in the background. © Coit Museum of Pharmacy & Health Sciences, The University of Arizona College of Pharmacy (used with permission)

Modern-day Upjohn products on display in the contemporary exhibit, along with information about pharmacy education at the University of Southern California below. © Coit Museum of Pharmacy & Health Sciences, The University of Arizona College of Pharmacy (used with permission)

While the apothecary exhibit exquisitely showcased history, the modern display room invited visitors to learn about present-day Upjohn. A transparency covered an entire wall of this room, showing the company's Portage Road manufacturing plant, just outside Kalamazoo. The image was illuminated one section at a time, while a voice recording explained what happened in that area of the plant. Four rotating rectangular columns in the middle of the room acted as a timeline of Upjohn's manufacturing process. Synchronized with the Portage plant voice-over, the first column represented research; the second, clinical research; the third, production; and the fourth, distribution. A large display case nearby boasted many current Upjohn products, from Cebenase to Zymacap to Cheracol. In total, there were over 800 Upjohn products on display throughout the store.

Though it was certainly never the main attraction of Disneyland, a visit to the Upjohn Pharmacy was an experience in its own right. It was an intricately crafted, multisensory environment that offered a glimpse into the past, present, and future of pharmacy.

Upjohn on Main Street

"Unsurprisingly, major corporations represented in Disneyland... were from sectors of industry identified with post-World War II economic growth, whose contribution to and promotion of consumerism was essential in shaping new ways of life." (Clément 2018)

The Upjohn Pharmacy's location on a corner of Main Street, U.S.A., was part of Walt Disney's larger notion of turn-of-the-century Anytown, U.S.A. Inspired by his boyhood memories of Marceline, Missouri, Main Street, U.S.A., conveyed an idealized vision of the past. Walt's goal was to bring back happy memories "for those... who remember the carefree times it recreates." Given that recent history had included two World Wars and the Great Depression, and given that the park itself was opening at a time when real-life small towns were on the decline in America, it is not surprising that Main Street, U.S.A., bore a certain whitewashed façade. The Disney company has not been afraid to admit this, either, calling it "quite unlike the real Main Streets of yesteryear." Author Mike Wallace writes, "Walt's approach to the past was not to reproduce it, but to *improve* it."

Fortuitously, the time period that Disney had re-created also recalled the early years of Upjohn itself. The company was founded in 1886, so its own history fit seamlessly into Disney's rendering of "the America of 1890-1910, at the crossroads of an era." Much like Disney's own journey from poverty to fortune, The Upjohn Company had come from humble beginnings. Its inception took place at a critical point in the history of pharmacy, a period of roughly 35 years which can be considered the birth of the modern drug industry.

Tied into the Second Industrial Revolution, the latter half of the 19th century saw the founding of hundreds of drug companies, including many that would go on to become industry titans. At the time, drugs and their production methods were quite rudimentary (the shift from dingy apothecaries to modern science was still decades away), but this period laid the groundwork for what was to come. Below is a timeline of some of the major drugmakers that were established during these years:

- 1853 - McKesson & Robbins
- 1858 - E. R. Squibb
- 1860 - Sharp & Dohme

- 1860 - John Wyeth & Brother
- 1863 - Burroughs Wellcome & Company
- 1866 - Parke, Davis & Company
- 1875 - Smith, Kline & Company
- 1876 - Eli Lilly & Company
- 1885 - Johnson & Johnson
- 1886 - The Upjohn Company
- 1888 - Abbott Laboratories

The Upjohn Company was founded by William Erastus Upjohn (1853-1932), the ninth child of Uriah (1808-1896) and Maria Mills Upjohn (1821-1882).[21] Uriah, a respected physician, had worked hard to instill an interest in medicine in his children, and many of them followed in his professional footsteps.[22]

Uriah was a Michigan pioneer and a leader in his community. For 20 years of his medical practice, he would travel on horseback around the counties of Kalamazoo, Allegan, Barry, Calhoun, and St. Joseph, tending to the sick. He would frequently be gone for days at a time, often receiving no pay for his services except for perhaps some food for himself and his horse. Later in his life, Uriah would help to establish the Kalamazoo County Medical Society, work to protect the locals from a deadly typhoid epidemic, and use his political influence to speak out against slavery.

Young William Upjohn, Uriah's son and the future founder of The Upjohn Company, completed his medical degree in 1875, but his big breakthrough came a decade later. He was an inventive type—no stranger to tinkering[23]—and he set out to develop a machine that could produce pills. Little could he have imagined that this pet project, done independently and in secret, would change pharmacy forever.

Prior to this time, pills were made almost exclusively by hand; the process was time-consuming, laborious, and highly inexact.[24] Upjohn family historian Richard Light describes the pill-making process and explains how William's invention worked:

> At that time doctors were still making pills by mixing dry ingredients into bread-like dough, rolling it thin, cutting it into small cubes which were rolled by hand into pellets, then baking them in the oven. Although Parke Davis,[25] one of the earliest drug companies, had mechanized the process, the resultant products were similar to the hand-rolled pellets. The Upjohn invention used a totally different principle. In a large open-faced rotating drum, tilted at 45 degrees, small grains of sugar were sent rolling in a random tumble. When

> the active pharmaceutical ingredients were slowly added, together with small amounts of water, the drug bound to the sugar crystals. Inert ingredients were then added to build up the size of the pill. The result was growth by accretion, much as snowballs grow when rolled downhill. This method possessed three advantages over the hand-processed pills: The resulting pill was friable and the fragments were quickly absorbed, it permitted mass production, and it provided uniform dosage.

These "friable" pills were a revolutionary innovation—in every way, they were superior to what had come before. Traditional hand-rolled pills were very hard and sometimes even coated in compounds like silver, which meant that they were difficult for the human body to absorb and therefore had little, if any therapeutic effect.[26] Upjohn's pills, on the other hand, could be "reduced to a powder under the thumb," as the company's branding would soon state.[27] In practice, this meant that they could be absorbed quickly and provide faster relief than other drugs on the market.

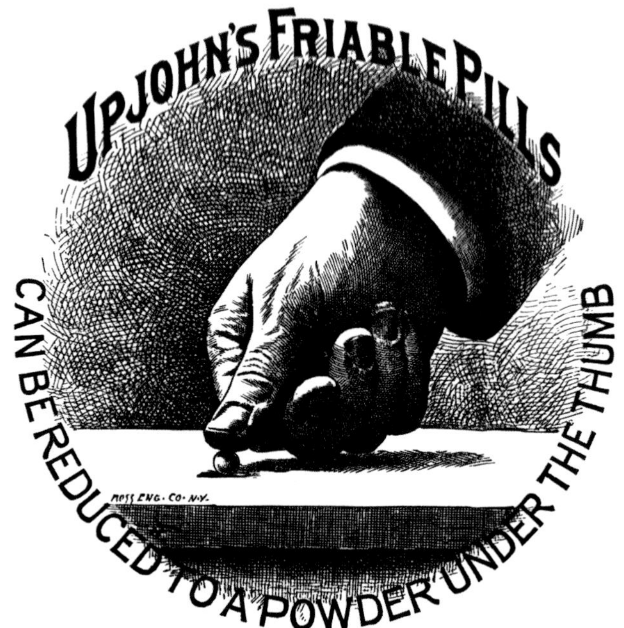

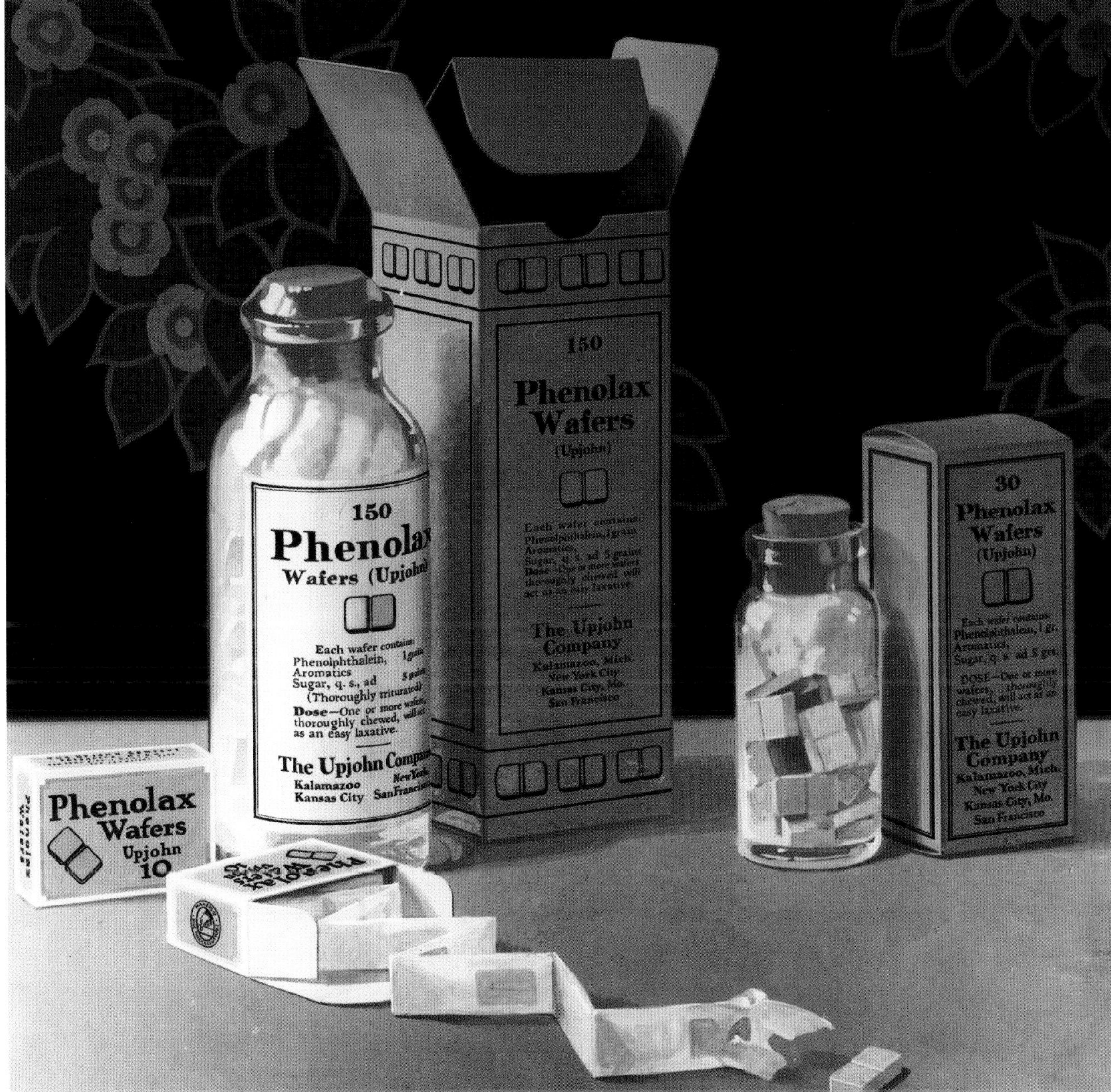

Phenolax Advertisement, ca. 1910s/1920s, undated. Donald Reid Parfet / The Upjohn Company Collection, privately held, Kalamazoo, Michigan.

Previous page top: One version of The Upjohn Company's friable pill/ thumb logo, undated. Donald Reid Parfet / The Upjohn Company Collection, privately held, Kalamazoo, Michigan.

Previous page bottom: The other version of The Upjohn Company's friable pill/thumb logo, undated. Donald Reid Parfet / The Upjohn Company Collection, privately held, Kalamazoo, Michigan.

One of the former Upjohn buildings in downtown Kalamazoo still bears the company name today. © Stephen Hall

Photograph (aerial) of The Upjohn Company's downtown Kalamazoo campus, pre-1990. Donald Reid Parfet / The Upjohn Company Collection, privately held, Kalamazoo, Michigan.

The Upjohn Pill and Granule Company, as it was originally called, began as a small-scale family operation run out of a Kalamazoo basement, but soon grew to be an important player in the drug industry.[28] Just 14 years after its founding, the company's catalog featured more than 700 items! Thus, Disneyland afforded Upjohn the perfect opportunity to insert its own story into a utopian, small-town narrative—if Main Street, U.S.A., was "a perpetually active and exciting place" and it represented traditional American values and ideals, then where better for a major company to present itself as the quintessential American entity?

Despite Disneyland being a promising staging area for Upjohn's marketing, however, the company still had to reconcile its nostalgic look at the past with its desire to present itself as a cutting-edge, forward-thinking changemaker.

Fortunately for the early lessees of Main Street, U.S.A., Walt Disney had next to no experience in the retail industry. It is partially for this reason that companies like Upjohn were invited to be a part of Disneyland in the first place. As author Dave Mason writes:

> Disney was a specialist in storytelling. He knew that it would take time for his new management team to learn the art of merchandising on [a large]

> scale, and he needed experienced partners to meet the expectations of a worldwide customer base that understood and appreciated his commitment to the finest in quality.

Even companies that did not sponsor a physical storefront were happy to be represented throughout the park. By making their products available in "the American West" of Frontierland or the old-time restaurants of Main Street, U.S.A., brands like PepsiCo and Frito-Lay could associate themselves with American traditions. How much more, then, could brands like Maxwell House, Carnation, and Upjohn, whose names were emblazoned in bright lights on the park's main thoroughfare, stand to benefit from multisensory, experiential advertisements?

One writer proposes a set of four criteria that may have helped to determine which companies would be chosen as Disneyland's lessees:

1. Companies whose wares, services, or brand image were a good fit with the land's theme
2. Companies whose expertise was needed for running the park or supplying content
3. Companies that were prosperous enough not to mind the high costs of running an operation in Disneyland
4. Companies who would not compete with other corporations already present in the park

Upjohn squarely met all these criteria:

1. The neighborhood drugstore was an iconic piece of Americana—the heart of many an American town—so it was a natural choice for Main Street, U.S.A.
2. Since the Disney Company likely had no knowledge of pharmacy history, it looked to Upjohn to supply appropriate content, and even yielded to its expertise when designing the physical storefront.
3. The Upjohn Company was certainly prosperous—its sales volume had steadily increased every year for the previous three decades.
4. Lastly, with no competitor companies present in Disneyland, Upjohn acted as the sole representation of the pharmaceutical industry.

Although the Upjohn store had nothing for sale, it still fit into Disney's larger merchandising schema with its branded promotional freebies. It was also not the only shop that lacked merchandise; elsewhere on Main Street, U.S.A., an operational

Bank of America branch sold no products, but offered special money orders printed exclusively for Disneyland. (Like the shopkeepers at the Upjohn Pharmacy, the bank associates wore proper period costumes.)

Main Street, U.S.A., was crafted to juxtapose 19th- and 20th-century life, and its design drew heavily upon the mise-en-scène of classic "small-town" movies like *It's a Wonderful Life*, *Our Town*, and *Love Finds Andy Hardy*. In each of these films, the local drugstore is a key part of the town's culture, what author Robert Neuman calls "the chief socializing locus for people of all ages" and "the American ideal of community."

As a filmmaker himself, Walt Disney had a keen eye for set design, so he undoubtedly recognized the importance of the Upjohn Pharmacy to his vision of Main Street, U.S.A. The Upjohn Company was not in the retail drug business, of course, but that did not seem to matter; by aligning itself with the retail industry in one of the most public spaces in the world, the company was able to cash in on the warm feelings evoked by small town memories.

Author Stephen Fjellman writes that Disney's vision of America "taps into people's nostalgic need for a false history." By inviting store visitors to remember the "good old days," The Upjohn Company positioned itself to subsume their memories and insert itself into a collective, pseudo-historical experience. For the rest of a patron's life, anytime he or she reminisced about a friendly neighborhood drugstore, The Upjohn Company would be there by association. (This notion extends to the store's contemporary exhibit, as well. Given that the average layman likely knew little about pharmacy, a visit to the Upjohn store would make The Upjohn Company symbolic of the entire industry in patrons' minds.)

Walt Disney wanted to capture a particular moment, a time when, as he put it, "the gas lamp is gradually being replaced by the electric lamp," and "the plodding, horse-drawn streetcar is giving way to the chugging 'horseless carriage.'" Upjohn embraced this inter-century mentality, using the pharmacy's historical and modern exhibits to showcase its own "then and now."

Playing to visitors' nostalgia for (supposedly) simpler times and their curiosity for New Age innovation, the Upjohn Pharmacy was both warmly familiar and excitingly futuristic. It was part of an idealized Main Street, U.S.A., that was better than the real turn-of-the-century Main Streets ever could have been.

Small Shops vs. Big Business

"Somewhere in 1949 or 1950, The Upjohn Company crossed the threshold into the era of modern pharmaceuticals. No one event signaled that passage, no memo marked the date. Yet the basic change happened in those months. From then on, Upjohn was outward bound toward the worldwide enterprise it is today." (Carlisle 1987: 101)

If Main Street, U.S.A., could be thought of as a microcosm of America (or at least an idealized version of it), then the Upjohn Pharmacy could be thought of as a microcosm of the larger pharmacy industry, viewed, of course, through the Upjohn lens. Like America had been at the turn of the century, the pharmacy profession was at a "crossroads" of its own at the time Disneyland opened.

In the decades prior, the notion of the "corner drugstore" had been well-established in the American idiom. One author calls them "uniquely American," places that "cater to the especially American quest for well-being." Historically, pharmacies were congenial places, where family and townsfolk came together, and by 1900, they acted as the health and communication centers of most neighborhoods. In an article about the Upjohn Pharmacy, *The Disneyland News* called drugstores "one of the most prominant [*sic*] landmarks of any small American town or village." A mixture of science and sociability, drugstores were places where gossip would be shared, sundries purchased, and tasty treats consumed. The early stores had a distinct personality about them. Author Jane Mobley writes:

> [Drugstores] were a little like the circus, full of surprises and contradictions. They were dark, pungent and mysterious in the pharmacy area, full of candy and treats up front, a tiny wonderland of crystal, exotic scents, books and valentines mixed up with utterly mundane necessaries like brooms and rat poison. For customers, the drug store promised that an errand could become an adventure.

At the turn of the century, there were over 46,000 pharmacists practicing across the U.S. As a comparison, for every one pharmacy in Europe at this time, there were eight in America. This may have been a result of the low barrier to entry—at the time, licensure typically required only an elementary education and a two-year pharmacy certification course.[29] Thus, with a few night classes, most anyone could practice pharmacy. It would not be until 1932 that a four-year college degree would be required for licensure.

However, the druggist's role was different during this period. Pharmacists practiced "counter-prescribing," which in some cases was more commonplace than filling actual prescriptions from a physician. Furthermore, pharmacists were on-call at all hours, which meant regularly tending to patients in the middle of the night for ailments that could not wait until the morning.

From a business perspective, turn-of-the-century drugstores were generally small-scale family operations. It was rare for an individual to own more than one store; by 1900, there were no more than 25 chain pharmacies in the country. By the time of the Great Depression, however, the drugstore industry was booming. In 1920, the U.S. had over 1,500 chain drugstores, and by 1929, this figure had more than doubled.

Numerous factors contributed to the growth of retail pharmacies. One was their frequent exemption from so-called "Blue Laws," which prohibited the sale of certain wares on Sundays. In many states across the country, pharmacies were permitted to sell on the Sabbath products like candy, soda water, and, most notably, cigars, when other businesses could not.

Another factor was the arrival of flapper fashion. As women's styles changed, makeup became more popular than ever and the demand for cosmetics grew significantly. To meet this demand, pharmacists (who at the time were almost exclusively men) began hiring women to work as sales representatives to appeal to the needs of an increasingly female clientele.

New product lines expanded far beyond just cosmetics, too. A widespread overhaul of wares meant more options for consumers and more profit for proprietors. Drugstores carried greeting cards, magazines, comic books, radios, small household appliances, phonographs, records, toys, and more. They were also among the first businesses to embrace the medium of photography—amateur shutterbugs relied on the chemicals and equipment they supplied.[30]

In addition to new wares on their shelves, as many as 60 percent of American pharmacies had soda fountains during Prohibition, which further cemented their status as social gathering places and alternatives to traditional taverns. Nationwide, soda fountains brought in as much as $1 million in revenue per day during the 1920s. As time went on, they became a ubiquitous icon of pharmacy in American culture.[31] Walt Disney himself had a working soda fountain, complete with a full backbar, at his Carolwood home in Holmby Hills, Los Angeles.[32] During the Depression, drugstores sold two things people really needed: health-related products and a bit of good cheer.

Within his own community of Kalamazoo, W. E. Upjohn made an effort to ease the pain of the Depression as well.[33] He purchased 1,700 acres of farmland in nearby Richland, with the goal of providing work to the unemployed and low-cost food to the destitute. "A day's wages might include a few precious dollars and an equally precious sack of potatoes," said an article about the company's history.

"Often the same bus that made the daily run to Kalamazoo to pick up the farm workers would also stop at a relief center or church to deliver foodstuffs to the needy."

All profits from the farm went to the W. E. Upjohn Unemployment Trustee Corporation, a nonprofit he created in 1932 to research the causes and effects of unemployment. Dr. Upjohn called the corporation, which was established just six weeks before his death, "the most important thing [he] ever did."

Historian Mickey Smith has written extensively about old-time depictions of pharmacists in popular media, from the on-screen portrayals of John Wayne and W. C. Fields to radio programs like *Fibber McGee and Molly* and *The Great Gildersleeve*. Both of the latter were broadcast until the mid-1950s, featuring recurring pharmacist and soda jerk characters in drugstore locales. Smith writes, "[T]he old radio types provide more than just entertainment. They also supply a view of the image of a pharmacist of the time."

Given the wide audience of these shows—*Fibber McGee* was the most popular radio program of its era—it seems safe to assume that many of the adults who visited Disneyland in the early days would have listened to them. These middle-class morality tales reinforced the idea of mom-and-pop drugstores as community hubs, where the kindly pharmacist had time for conversation and for involvement in the personal affairs of his neighbors. (As an aside, it does not seem to matter whether this rosy notion had real, historical foundation or not. When it came to the Upjohn Pharmacy, the image of the druggist as a friendly neighborhood everyman fit perfectly into Disney's utopian vision of America.)

Upjohn itself echoed these sentiments. In its article announcing the opening of the Upjohn Pharmacy, *Scope* magazine said of the period it re-created, "Drugs may not have been as potent then as they are today, but this was largely compensated for by the proprietor's friendliness and willingness to render a service beyond the requirements of a commercial transaction."

Contrary to this, however, the mid-20th century saw marked changes throughout the pharmacy profession. On the retail side, Walgreens had moved toward a "Super Store" model post-World War II, and by 1953, it had become the largest self-service chain in the country. The company's own centennial history admits, "In the postwar years, the line between drugstores and department stores was blurring." Convenience, rather than community, had become the key concept in retail pharmacy.

This holds true for Rexall, as well, which saw a great deal of corporate turbulence in the 1950s. Several years prior, under new leadership, Rexall had closed dozens of small, company-owned stores in favor of mega-retail spaces. By 1950, Rexall was losing money, and, though it bounced back by the end of the decade, things had changed, and the company had arguably lost its sense of "family spirit."

As the competitive retail environment rapidly shifted, pharmacies also had to contend with outside pressures. By 1937, 75 percent of supermarkets had drug and cosmetic departments, and shortly thereafter, discount drug chains came on the scene, adding an entirely new form of competition.

On the educational side, pharmacy was moving away from traditional apprenticeship training and toward a model of collegiate education. Colleges of pharmacy had existed in the U.S. since 1821, but it took many years for them to become truly widespread, particularly in the west.[34]

In 1900, 21 U.S. pharmacy schools organized to form the American Conference of Pharmaceutical Faculties.[35] This organization sought to push pharmacy education forward and to establish educational standards for students. (However, apprenticeship training continued to be a legitimate path to the profession for almost three decades. It was not until 1929 that the national standard was officially changed to require pharmacists to have a Bachelor of Science degree,[36] a change that essentially killed apprenticeship training altogether.)

On the professional side, the practice of pharmacy was expanding as well. No longer were pharmacists just small-town drugstore owners. New developments in science meant new opportunities for practitioners, so the first half of the 20th century saw pharmacists working in new capacities like research, sales, and drug development.

Among the most significant changes was the growth of hospital pharmacy. Though the roots of this practice in America can be traced as far back as the colonial era, it did not become a significant movement until the 1920s.[37] In prior decades, hospital pharmacy was a small branch of the profession, mostly limited to Catholic nuns working in religious hospitals.

In the 19th century, there were only a handful of drugs that might have been prescribed in a hospital, so physicians could generally handle the responsibility of dispensing by themselves. As new classes of drugs came to market, however, it became more and more necessary to employ specialists with formal training and a focused, intricate knowledge of them. It should come as no surprise, therefore, that hospital pharmacy's rise took place alongside developments in pharmaceutical education and drug discovery—it was intertwined with both of them.[38]

On the research and development side, changes were also happening at an unprecedented rate. The same year Disneyland opened its gates, the polio vaccine was introduced and Tylenol was brought to market. According to Upjohn's centennial history, postwar research had become "a fast, tense race throughout the industry." Half the drugs prescribed in 1953 did not exist 10 years earlier, and 90 percent did not exist 15 years earlier.

Less than a year after Disneyland opened, Upjohn introduced Albamycin, its first major antibiotic. Shortly thereafter, the compound was reformulated to produce Panalba, which quickly became one of the most-prescribed antibiotics on the market. Its demand was so extraordinary that Upjohn had to cease much of its other production just to meet it. Similarly, Upjohn's diabetes drug Orinase received FDA approval in 1957, and by the end of the decade, a third of diabetics in the United States were using it daily.

It is worth pausing here to note that these developments within The Upjohn Company happened, in large part, because of Donald Gilmore's leadership and business acumen. As one author put it:

> Although Donald Gilmore lacked medical training, he became a dominating force at Upjohn… [he] foresaw the contribution of research in the pharmaceutical industry. Under his direction during World War II, the company increased production of penicillin and heparin, which saved thousands of lives and kept the company from going bankrupt as over 3,500 other drug companies did."

During World War II, Upjohn worked closely with the United States government to aid the Allied forces. Like many other pharmaceutical companies, it devoted significant research efforts to the development of wartime drugs. At least 87 Upjohn products—likely more—saw military use, including penicillin, serum albumin, and sulfanilamide. These and other compounds played a central role in the outcome of the conflict.

Beginning in 1941, much of Upjohn's production capacity was devoted to the armed forces. Throughout the war, it produced upwards of $14 million worth of medical supplies at cost. At one point, the company received an order from the U.S. government for more than 130 million tablets of a single drug![39] Upjohn's involvement in the home-front effort undoubtedly helped to shape its image as a proud American company, an image it would later try to build on in Disneyland.

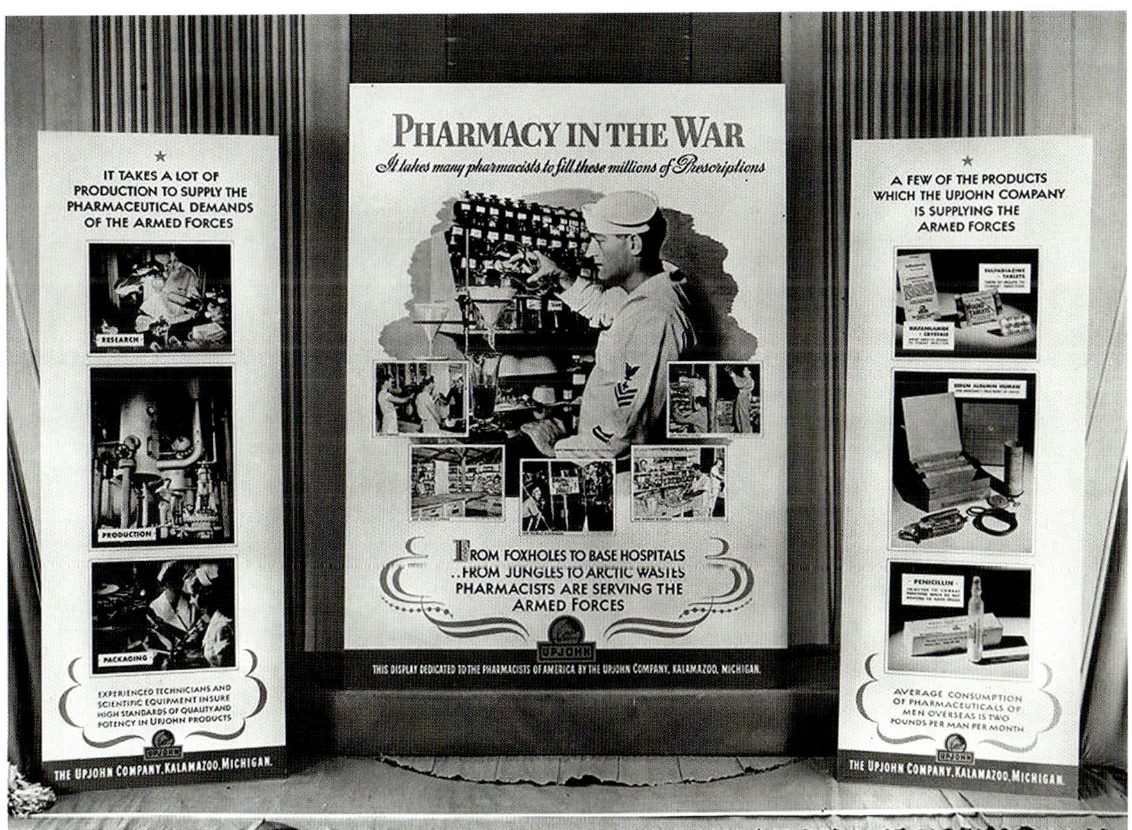

Left: Informational advertisements promoting Upjohn's contributions to the war effort.
© The Upjohn Company (used under fair use)

Below: Upjohn's sulfadiazine tablets, manufactured in sliding plastic cases that were able to be opened by "a wounded man denied the use of an arm."
© The Upjohn Company (used under fair use)

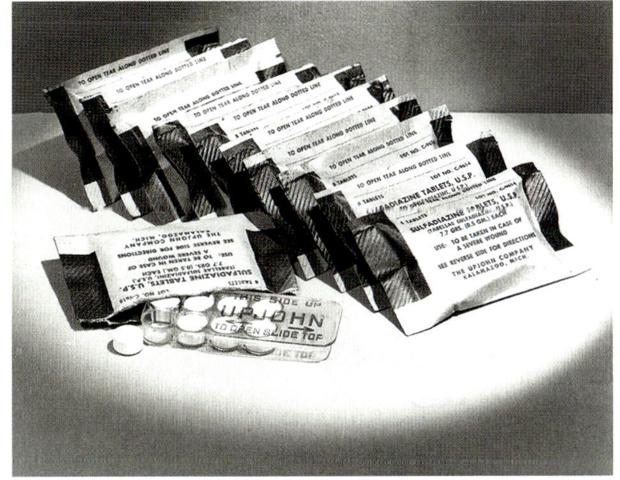

Above: Upjohn's Frank Holmes and Howard Weatherwax raise the Army-Navy flag at Upjohn's headquarters in downtown Kalamazoo, November 24, 1944.

Page 63: Upjohn's "Building 41" under construction in Kalamazoo, March 24, 1948. Both images © The Upjohn Company (used under fair use)

In addition to paradigm-altering changes in the pharmaceutical sciences, drug companies themselves were evolving as never before. Corporate acquisitions and mergers like that of Merck with Sharp & Dohme are too numerous to list. Millions upon millions of dollars were being poured into research, and companies were doubling or tripling in size seemingly overnight.

Within Upjohn itself, in 1945, the company's operations were housed in 30 buildings, but their combined 838,000 square feet of space was still not sufficient. Estimates predicted the need for at least 40 percent more square footage, a need that led to the establishment of the Portage plant.[40] In 1951, a mammoth 33-acre space known as "Building 41" opened in Portage, which housed most of Upjohn's production from then on. That year, the company's research team nearly doubled in size. By 1953, Upjohn employed more than 4,200 people and held over 200 active patents. The company had also gone international by this point, holding subsidiary presences in England and Canada.

Simply put, Disneyland and the Upjohn Pharmacy opened at a time when the field of pharmacy looked fundamentally different than it ever had before. As a new era dawned amidst a barrage of exciting changes, the field shifted from nostalgic, corner drugstores to big business and hard science.

ENGINEERS BUILDERS
THE AUSTIN METHOD
NAME UPJOHN CO. (MANUFACTURING)
CITY KALAMAZOO MICH. SIZE 875 x 1140
CONT. NO. 3144 PHOTO DATE 3-24-48 NO. 50

Yesterday, Today and (Mostly) Tomorrow

"[Walt Disney] helped Americans define who they were by depicting where they had been and where they were going..." (Francaviglia 1995: 72)

In light of unprecedented changes in pharmacy, it is worth examining the periods in which the first Disneyland visitors were born. Of those who came to the park in the 1950s, one can assume that the younger visitors were born close to or during World War II, and their parents were likely children of the Depression, many of whom doubtless served in the war.

In terms of pharmacy's timeline, these two generations fall on either side of the massive changes discussed previously. The adults would have grown up around classic drugstores, but these were quickly phasing out during their children's developmental years. Compared to the real, operational pharmacies of 1955, the Upjohn Pharmacy would have felt like a throwback to adults, and a sort of recent-history lesson to children.

With so much nostalgia for the "good old days," it seems worthwhile to consider, in terms of actual science, just how "good" they really were. For the 19th-century physician, patient care mostly consisted of primitive procedures and crude remedies made from herbs and plants.

So-called "patent medicines" flourished from the 1870s to the 1930s. These concoctions fed a widespread desire for quick-fix miracle cures as an alternative to prescription drugs and painful medical/surgical procedures. Given that these drugs frequently contained compounds like heroin, morphine, cocaine, opium, cannabis, and chloroform, it goes without saying that they likely had no effect on the diseases they were advertised to cure, and in many cases were downright dangerous or even deadly. (Amusingly though, the notion of a quack doctor peddling boozy snake oils has become a well-known and well-loved part of medico-historical lore.)

A mixture of devious advertising, egregious claims, and general mystery made patent medicines attractive to consumers. Their names frequently included terms like "Indian," "Persian," or "French"—the more "exotic" a product sounded, the more legitimate the public often believed it to be. Ironically, though, these elixirs were usually made by white promoters and contained few, if any ingredients from other cultures. The makers of these drugs would offer lowball pricing, but would in turn use subpar ingredients. Particularly in the case of a traveling medicine show, by the time a patient realized a drug was useless (if they realized it at all), the salesman would have already been long gone.

Multiple factors contributed to patent medicines' rise, but perhaps the most fundamental was the population's relative lack of medical knowledge. With a flood of low-quality drugs on the market, patients had little protection from them besides requesting reputable products by name from their local druggist. However, doing so would have required both knowledge of these products and the ability to differentiate them from illegitimate drugs. Historian A. Walker Bingham writes:

> There are recorded cases by the hundreds of the drastic effects of [patent medicines] on the unsuspecting, particularly the very young. No amount of nostalgia can gloss over the horrors that were committed knowingly and unknowingly by placing lethal preparations in the hands of an unsophisticated public.

These horrors did not go unnoticed. In 1905 and 1906, Samuel Hopkins Adams, a muckraker and contemporary of Upton Sinclair, wrote a series of scathing articles in *Collier's Weekly* entitled *The Great American Fraud*, in which he lambasted the patent medicine industry and its practices. The series' opening paragraph reads:

> Gullible America will spend this year some seventy-five [million] dollars in the purchase of patent medicines. In consideration of this sum it will swallow huge quantities of alcohol, an appalling amount of opiates and narcotics, a wide assortment of varied drugs ranging from powerful and dangerous heart depressants to insidious liver stimulants; and, far in excess of all other ingredients, undiluted fraud.

Consumers' reliance on sham remedies as a substitute for legitimate medical care was itself a major issue, but it was exacerbated by their willingness to self-dose. Patent drugs frequently made misleading or false claims, which instilled misplaced confidence in their efficacy and encouraged improper use (more improper than simply taking them in the first place). Cocaine, for example, was originally touted as a nonaddictive pain reliever, a claim that undoubtedly led to addiction and overdosing.

Adams' treatise addressed these issues as they were happening, noting that compounds such as cocaine and opium were "concealed in the 'cough remedies,' 'soothing syrups,' and 'catarrhal powders' of which they [were] the basis."

It was not until the Pure Food and Drug Act of 1906—a piece of legislation largely owed to critics like Adams and Sinclair—that manufacturers were required to list the quantities of compounds like alcohol and opium in their products.[41] This landmark law was responsible for the creation of the Food & Drug Administration, but its timing meant that for the better part of the period Main Street, U.S.A. re-created—that romantically nostalgic era of supposed innocence—the drug industry had essentially no oversight. Dangerous snake oils ran rampant and caused untold harm.[42]

What's more, the Pure Food and Drug Act was only the beginning of modern consumer safety regulation. Subsequent acts and amendments followed over the next decades, such as the Sherley Amendment of 1912, which prohibited the labeling of drug products with false or misleading claims, and more significantly, the Food, Drug, and Cosmetic Act of 1938, which required manufacturers to prove a drug safe to use before it could be sold. (The latter essentially replaced the original 1906 law, which by that point had become obsolete.)

The Food, Drug, and Cosmetic Act was a direct result of the so-called "Sulfanilamide Disaster" of 1937. In June of that year, a salesman for the pharmaceutical firm S.E. Massengill Co. reported demand for a liquid form of sulfanilamide, a drug used to treat streptococcal infections. Massengill chemists immediately got to work and soon discovered that the drug dissolved in a compound called diethylene glycol. In order to meet demand quickly, and with no regulations in place to require testing to ensure safety and efficacy, the company sent out hundreds of shipments of its new product without delay. Because there had been no pharmacological testing done on it, however, the chemists failed to realize that diethylene glycol is a deadly poison. (Today, it is used as an antifreeze.) As a result of their negligence, over 100 people in 15 states died after ingesting the lethal concoction.

Though patent medicines had caused widespread issues long before 1937, the Sulfanilamide Disaster was the final straw that led to updated legislation.[43]

Even as the pharmaceutical industry saw increased oversight during the first half of the 20th century, by the mid-century it faced new challenges on multiple fronts. Serious concerns were being raised about the ethics of drug marketing, which led to congressional hearings. Additionally, with so many new types of drugs being brought to market—drugs which cost millions of research dollars to produce—the rapidly rising cost of prescription medications became a major issue.

To the credit of The Upjohn Company, since its inception, it had striven for quality and efficacy, despite there being no legal mandate to do so for the first 20 years of its existence. The *Journal of the American Pharmaceutical Association* once said of Upjohn's early years:

> Although the Food, Drug, and Cosmetic Act and other government protection for the consumer were still far in the future, and many a manufacturer made his fortune by adulteration, Dr. Upjohn posted signs all around his little plant, "Keep the Quality Up—W. E. Upjohn."[44]

This phrase would remain the company's motto for the rest of its life. Rather than sell low-grade drugs at cut-rate prices, Dr. Upjohn's philosophy was to let the quality of his products speak for itself.

Geographically, the American West—the eventual home of Disneyland—had a population particularly susceptible to illness. Arizona and California were the primary havens for tuberculosis patients, but in their rugged environments, medical personnel were scarce. (In 1881, the Arizona territory had only eight druggists!) On top of this, the available curative methods were typically crude and painful. Historian Robert Kravetz writes:

> During the early days of the Western frontier it was not at all uncommon for the town doctor to also fill the role of town druggist.[45] A doctor would often open a drugstore as a source of extra income and to serve as a base of operation for his medical practice. Local residents would frequently use the store as a communication center, leaving messages tacked to the front door requesting urgent assistance for some injury or illness.

At the turn of the century, at least 20 percent of those who emigrated to the Southwest were invalids in search of a healthful climate and a better life. In 1910, as the sick poured in from all over the country, tuberculosis was responsible for one in seven deaths in California.

With all this turmoil in the preceding decades, The Upjohn Company naturally took some creative liberties to ensure that its Disneyland store remained family friendly. This was in keeping with Walt Disney's broader view of the past; Disneyland was (and still is) awash with nostalgia, providing a sanitized view of history for its guests. This was certainly the case for Upjohn's depiction of pharmacy history—had the company portrayed things more accurately, its Disneyland store might have included references to alcohol, cocaine, disease, and death!

Just as the old cure-all nostrums were fictitious in their claims of effectiveness, so too was Upjohn's portrayal of a past in which the field of pharmacy was without issue.

Many authors have analyzed the impact that Disney parks have on visitors' understanding of national identity. "Indeed, Disney theme parks are some of the foremost places where the nation consumes its collective memory of the American experience and the American national narrative," writes historian Bethanee Bemis. "After all, Disney is in the business of selling memories. Not just memories of family vacations, but memories of stories from American history."

The Upjohn Pharmacy was just one piece of what she calls a "happily nostalgic kingdom of American myth," and though its selective presentation of the past could be seen as problematic, The Upjohn Company's rationale for excluding certain aspects of history is entirely understandable from a business perspective. The last thing Upjohn would have wanted would be to present content that visitors might find objectionable or that might associate its products with illegitimate medicine.

On the one hand, the omission of topics like addiction and quackery could be viewed as historical revisionism, but on the other hand, neither Disney nor Upjohn ever sought to create a pinpoint-accurate representation of the past. Just as no Disneyland visitors would ever mistake Main Street, U.S.A., for an actual Midwestern town, neither would they have mistaken the Upjohn Pharmacy for an actual 1890s apothecary. Indeed, Upjohn worked extensively to make the store look period-accurate, but its fundamental goal was always marketing, not historical education.

As the years went on and "big pharma" took hold, Upjohn's replica apothecary shop probably felt more and more foreign to visitors, particularly children. Concurrently, its modern display likely felt more relevant, as it spoke to a shifting cultural landscape by presenting cutting-edge research in a futuristic manner. Even during its brief, 15-year life span, the Upjohn Pharmacy seems to have steadily narrowed its focus toward modern science. Given the rapid changes happening throughout the pharmacy profession at that time, this makes sense.

By 1958, the Upjohn Pharmacy was due for refurbishment. Walt Disney made a trip to Kalamazoo[46] to confer with Donald Gilmore and other Upjohn executives about major renovations.

A central issue that The Upjohn Company hoped to address involved the store's open-door connection to the adjacent Main Street, U.S.A., Candle Shop. Since it adjoined the antiques exhibit, patrons' natural traffic patterns meant that they would frequently miss the modern display room altogether. Upjohn was concerned that if visitors only saw the apothecary shop, it would send the wrong message. A company memo said, "Too many people... seemed to think the company as well as the pharmacy was a thing of the past." Store manager Leo Austin proposed the construction of a glass case containing "appropriate material," positioned to channel visitors into the modern exhibit without obstructing their view of the candle shop.

Walt Disney waves as he disembarks at the Kalamazoo Airport. © Gilmore Car Museum (used with permission)

Left: Walt Disney visits Building 88 at Upjohn's Portage Plant near Kalamazoo, accompanied by Donald Gilmore. © Gilmore Car Museum (used with permission)

Lower left: Walt Disney tours the boardroom of Building 88 at Upjohn's Portage Plant. © Gilmore Car Museum (used with permission)

Below: Donald Gilmore wears a button that reads "I'm Goofy about Disneyland" at an Upjohn Company luncheon. Walt Disney passed out similar buttons to the Upjohn officials who showed him around the Portage plant that day. © Gilmore Car Museum (used with permission)

Right: Walt Disney converses with Upjohn executives in the dining room of Building 88. © Gilmore Car Museum (used with permission)

Left: Walt Disney entertains local children at the Kalamazoo Art Center.
© Gilmore Car Museum (used with permission)

Above: Walt Disney during a visit to the Portage plant.
© Gilmore Car Museum (used with permission)

Walt Disney during a visit to the Portage plant. © Gilmore Car Museum (used with permission)

Walt Disney inspects a classic car at Gilmore Car Museum. © Gilmore Car Museum (used with permission)

Walt Disney and Donald Gilmore outside at the Gilmore Car Museum. © Gilmore Car Museum (used with permission)

Walt Disney sits at the coffee table in Donald Gilmore's cottage at Gull Lake. © Gilmore Car Museum (used with permission)

In order to further drive home the message of a rapidly changing industry, and to present Upjohn as the bellwether of change, the refurbishment plan suggested further distinction between the store's two exhibits. It read, "[A]n even more decisive delineation could be drawn between the antique section and the modern section. The separation in time is not as crystal clear as it should be to be most effective."

The store's Upjohn products display was periodically updated to showcase the company's newest offerings. Employee H. S. Cripe humorously described the display case's need for a "productectomy," and told of how "[a] realignment of the shelves, a redistribution of the products selected, and the inclusion of a card explaining the case brought the patient well along on the road to recovery."

Around 1959, the Upjohn Pharmacy exhibited Will Burtin's six-foot model of "The Cell," one of the life-sized scientific displays Upjohn had commissioned him to create. In keeping with the modern exhibit's futuristic mentality and Burtin's own sci-fi

Upper left: Walt Disney, alongside Sue and Pete Parish, smiles at a young boy while handing Sue something he just signed. Taken during a reception for Disney at the Gilmore Car Museum. © Gilmore Car Museum (used with permission)

Lower left: A group from Upjohn stands in front of the company's hangar at the Kalamazoo Airport to see Walt Disney off. © Gilmore Car Museum (used with permission)

aesthetic, this kinetic display was dramatically lighted from within in shades of buff, red, green, and blue.[47] Walt Disney himself was said to have been very complimentary of it.

Burtin's cell model has been described as a large domed web of clear plastic tubes, lit by pulsating lighting below and shined up through holes, causing the whole structure to glow rhythmically. In a version of the model that was four times larger than the one in Disneyland, visitors could enter and move about the cell, walking on a mirrored floor that appeared to turn its hemispherical structure into a full sphere.[48]

Burtin's unique approach to scientific visualization allowed Upjohn to build an identity as a company invested in community education. Given that the general populace was the audience of the Upjohn Pharmacy, it makes sense why Burtin's model was such a natural inclusion there. It was dynamic, eye-catching, and highly informative, and it built on the public's existing Atomic Age interest in science.

Over time, modern sensibilities crept into the Upjohn Pharmacy's antiques exhibit, as well. In the late 1950s, a display window at the back of the store was redeveloped to feature a short-lived male and female anatomy exhibit. An interoffice memo from Upjohn said:

> When [the anatomy exhibit] was installed, I heard, it caused the nearest thing to a furor ever seen on Main Street. As a result the two introductory panels were removed... Possible alternatives to this could be an exhibit showing the growth of the company through pictures of the buildings since its founding or an exhibit showing the world-wide scope of company operations.

From the get-go, the Upjohn store also promoted education and careers in pharmacy. In one of the earliest issues of *The Disneyland News*, Leo Austin stated, "We are here to promote Pharmacy and Pharmacutical [*sic*] Schools and the profession of Medicine."

Around 1961, still struggling to get visitors into the modern exhibit, a display was added that highlighted a "Pharmacy School of the Month," including information about academic programs and careers in the field. It seems that The Upjohn Company was trying to garner the attention of both adults—the visitors who had incomes and who might actually go on to purchase the products advertised in the store—and also their children, likely in hopes of sparking an interest in pharmacy and establishing brand identity in their minds. Perhaps as a way to support this initiative, Phil Harvey and W. G. Roberson, one of the later staff members

of the Upjohn Pharmacy, offered community lectures at the University of Southern California.

In 1966, Upjohn added another exhibit to its apothecary display. Though little information exists about its content, the company's annual report from that year described it as "dramatic," "[a trip] backward through time for 20,000 years for a close-up look at medical progress from nostrums and hexes to modern-day antibiotics and steroids."

The Upjohn Pharmacy's replica apothecary may have been the larger of its two exhibit spaces, but during its tenure in Disneyland, its parent company seems to have put increasingly more stake into its contemporary display.

Young guests view an exhibit at the Upjohn Pharmacy about alchemy and its historical connections to medicine. From the collection of davelandweb.com (used with permission).

The Other One

"[C. V. Wood] was clearly a con man and certainly behaved that way." (Quote from Disney Legend Bob Gurr, in Sampson 2010)

Once the vice president and general manager of Disneyland, Inc., Cornelius Vanderbilt "C. V." Wood would later be called "the most nefarious Disney villain of them all."

In 1954, Walt Disney hired C. V. Wood away from the Stanford Research Institute to help make Disneyland a reality. Wood played a crucial role in the park's development, from supervising the selection and purchase of the land in Anaheim to overseeing park operations during the first year. After a falling-out with Disney, however, Wood was ousted from the company. At that time, whether as a revenge tactic or merely an attempt to cash in on the popularity of Disney's park, Wood set out to make his own. The result was Freedomland U.S.A., an American-history-themed amusement park in New York's Bronx borough.

Wood's park borrowed heavily from Disneyland, so much so that during its short life span (1960-1964), it came to be known as "The Disneyland of the East." There are many parallels that can be drawn between the two parks, not the least of which involving their corporate sponsorships. Where Disneyland had the Carnation ice cream parlor, Freedomland had the Borden ice cream parlor. Where Disneyland had the Sunkist Citrus House, Freedomland had the Welch's Grape Juice bar.[49] And where Disneyland had the Upjohn Pharmacy, Freedomland had the Schering Apothecary.

Sponsored by the Schering Corporation, a significant player in the drug industry and a key competitor of Upjohn, this store was clearly a response to the Upjohn Pharmacy. It was part of Freedomland's re-creation of "Little Old New York," and it too was decorated with antique wares and designed to look like an old-time apothecary (though arguably not as faithfully as the Upjohn Pharmacy). The store's display pieces had been hand-picked from the private collection of Connecticut historian Sydney Blumberg. Of note were a leech jar and a mid-19th-century brass balance from France.

The *Journal of the American Pharmaceutical Association* called the store's antique collection "outstanding." Likewise, *Hospital Topics* said:

> Schering's display... shows the contrast between

The Schering Apothecary in Freedomland U.S.A.
Credit: Michael R. Virgintino Collection (used with permission)

medical [techniques] and equipment of 50 years ago and those of today. The exhibition consists of a mid-19th century apothecary shop, a display of the company's pharmaceutical research and production facilities, and a display showing career opportunities and requirements in health fields.

Just as visitors to the Upjohn Pharmacy received samples of Unicap vitamins, visitors to the Schering Apothecary received samples of the nasal decongestant Coricidin. Other promotional items were given to younger patrons, as well; boys received badges that read "Junior Scientist," and girls received nurses' caps and buttons that read "Nurse's Aid."

A sample packet of Coricidin, given out to guests at the Schering Apothecary in Freedomland U.S.A. Credit: Michael R. Virgintino Collection (used with permission)

The store's staff also passed out booklets about pharmacy careers. A clipping from an unidentified Schering publication states that the booklets had been prepared by the National Association of Chain Drug Stores to "urge students to choose the profession of pharmacy as a career." During the summer months, the store would employ students from nearby pharmacy schools to assist with operations and answer guests' questions.

It seems that Schering, like many drug companies at the time, was trying new marketing strategies. Having seen the success of the Upjohn Pharmacy, the company undoubtedly felt confident in its own ability to operate a similar, public-facing storefront.

When it came to advertising to pharmacists and physicians, Schering had an entire corps of detail men helping to spread its message. While its apothecary shop was in operation, Schering began a promotional campaign that would prove immensely successful among health professionals. Beginning in 1963, the company produced a series of commemorative mortars and pestles, most of which honored people or events in pharmacy's history. These premiums were given to doctors and druggists, and many were branded for Coricidin. The series remained so popular that new pieces were added almost every year until 2009, when Merck acquired Schering-Plough.

Schering mortar and pestle from 1963—the first of the series—with the pestle branded for Coricidin. © Stephen Hall

Though Freedomland never achieved nearly the renown of Disneyland, it still attracted a respectable number of patrons, especially early on. Following the park's opening, *The Billboard* estimated that 63,000 guests had shown up on opening day, and that 1.5 million more would visit in August 1960 alone.

The manager of the Schering Apothecary was Mr. Seymoure S. Fahrer, a longtime employee of the company. In an email to the author, his daughter, Toba Hartmann, shared her memories of the store:

> The exhibit was two rooms, the first outfitted as [an] old time apothecary, kind of dark, with a big see-through jar of leeches... [There were] pill rolling demonstrations, and all sorts of appropriate displays; the second room was smaller, light and modern, where the samples and buttons and fliers were handed out... Since they were giving out Coricidin samples to adults, the Apothecary was a living, breathing advertisement for Schering.

Hartmann's father oversaw store operations until Freedomland closed in September 1964. Afterward, he spent the rest of his career with Schering, eventually becoming the division manager for the Long Island area.

(Left to right) Toba Hartmann, Seymoure Fahrer, Helen Fahrer, and Diana Strayer at the Schering Apothecary in Freedomland U.S.A., 1961. Credit: Toba Hartmann collection (used with permission)

It is no surprise that Freedomland was designed to be an all-American destination, just as Disneyland was. With this in mind, it is ironic that unlike Upjohn, whose story began in America, Schering's story began in Germany, and its history is inseparably tied to that country's. Founded in the late 1920s, the Schering Corporation was an outgrowth of German drugmaker Schering AG, which had been founded decades earlier.[50]

Shortly after the company came to America, U.S.-Germany relations became strained as World War II tensions heated up. At the outset of the conflict, the United States government seized control of German properties in America, including those of Schering.

Between 1942 and 1945, Schering AG forced the slave labor of over 400 people in Germany. Decades later, when faced with criticism over its association with the German war machine, the company attempted to save face by noting that none of the laborers had come from concentration camps, and that they had been treated "better... than those at other companies." Around the same time as this public scrutiny, Schering AG was part of a lawsuit in which it was alleged that human experimentation in the camps had taken place with its "knowledge, consent and/or participation," and that its involvement had directly aided the Nazis.[51]

The U.S. arm of Schering would not completely separate from its German parent until 1952, a mere eight years before Freedomland opened. To his credit, C. V. Wood may not have known the ugly details of Schering's history, but since he sought to create a theme park that celebrated America and American innovation, Schering was certainly an odd choice of sponsor.

Six months after Freedomland closed, it was announced that a housing project would take its place.[52] Walt Disney himself had closely followed the operations of the rival park, and it seems that he learned from its downfall. Author Michael Virgintino writes:

> Many of the issues faced by Freedomland were revealed to Walt Disney during his involvement with the New York World's Fair. Though Walt had contemplated a northeast option for a new park, the various labor, construction and weather issues in the region, along with his personal experiences at the fair, convinced him to build in Florida.

Left: Seymoure Fahrer (center) speaks to students from Newfield High School in Selden, Long Island, inside the Schering Apothecary.
Credit: The Frank R. Adamo Freedomland U.S.A. Collection (used with permission)

Above: The Schering Apothecary in Freedomland U.S.A.
Credit: Toba Hartmann collection (used with permission)

Pharmacies in Marceline and Kansas City

"Those who knew Disney say he never forgot his early years in Marceline, for they were formative in developing his early character. His years in Marceline were relatively happy... Understandably, then, Walt Disney looked back on Marceline in particular, and the small town in general, with a great deal of nostalgia. It symbolized his youth and a freer—and perhaps fairer—time for him." (Francaviglia 1996: 145)

Since the town of Marceline, Missouri, was so instrumental in shaping Walt Disney's understanding of Americana, it stands to reason that its drugstores would have been instrumental in shaping his view of pharmacy. These stores and the druggists who owned them likely planted a seed in his mind; if Disney thought back on friendly neighborhood drugstores later in life, the stores he would have remembered would have likely been the ones in Marceline. By extension then, since the town provided the prototypical inspiration for Main Street, U.S.A., the drugstores that resided there arguably did the same for the Upjohn Pharmacy.

According to U.S. Census data, the population of Marceline township was 3,271 in 1900, and 4,572 in 1910. Given its small-town culture, it seems a safe bet that young Walt Disney knew many of the town's druggists. He likely visited their stores, enjoyed drinks at their soda fountains, and came to them for bandages when he scraped his knees playing outside.

An examination of Marceline's early drugstores reveals a surprisingly colorful, even shocking history. Published in 1912, six years after the Disney family moved there, the *Compendium of History and Biography of Linn County, Missouri* provides invaluable insight into the culture of early Marceline and its surrounding areas. The following is a lengthy but remarkable excerpt from this book (line breaks added for readability):

> Up to the period when Mayor Cash took the oath of office the city [of Marceline] was entirely without fire-fighting apparatus. Insurance rates were high, the fire record was bad and many of the first companies were closing up their agencies and withdrawing from the town... One of these early-day fires came near resulting

in the undoing of one of Marceline's pioneer physicians—Dr. J. T. Martin.

The doctor had come to the town with the first arrivals, hung out his sign as a practitioner and opened a drug store on the northeast corner of Kansas and California avenues. He was a studious man, an indefatigable investigator and being yet comparatively fresh from college was not ready to give up his researches into the mysteries of the anatomy of man. To more intelligently pursue his favorite subject he had procured a human body and had the cadaver reposing in his private study in the rear of the drug store awaiting a favorable opportunity to proceed with dissection at his leisure.

One night the doctor was called out to see a patient and his clerk having gone home, he locked up the drug store, put his medical case under his arm and was off to minister to his patient. His visit was a distant one and returning he saw a red glow in the vicinity of Marceline, and watching it curiously he rode along not specially concerned, for the reason that fires were not rare in Marceline...

Dr. Martin rode in all unsuspecting, and his amazement was sincere when he found his own drug store was in ashes. Meantime, the doctor, one of the most popular of men up to this time, was advised by his friends that he could not get away any too quickly if his personal safety was to be assured, as a mob was forming threatening serious bodily injury to him and the more excitable ones were talking lynching.

In answer to his excited inquiries, the doctor was informed that when the flames broke out in the roof of his building, people rushed to the spot, and not finding him there, broke into the building with a view to saving his library and other personal belongings. Among the first articles they uncovered was the cadaver, and as it offered no explanation of its presence, the cry was raised that the doctor was a grave robber, and excitement and indignation was at fever heat.

The physician was persuaded by his friends to remain away until explanations could be forthcoming and excitement subside. This he did, and he produced evidence to convince his neighbors not only that he was not a murderer or a ghoul, but that he had come into possession of the cadaver legally and honorably, and so at the end of forty-eight hours the doctor returned to Marceline, hung his sign again and the incident passed. His anatomical specimen, however, perished, as did his library and other office belongings, for every man who had rushed to that fire imbued with the idea of unselfishly saving Dr. Martin's property, had business elsewhere as soon as he caught a glimpse of the figure reclining on the doctor's sofa.

This incident was in 1889 and was followed in 1894 by one very similar in first appearances, but of vastly different results. Dr. [Richard] Fox was conducting a drug store at the corner of Kansas and Gracia avenues and had an ice box back of his prescription case. One day the dealer was delivering ice to the doctor and noticed the lid was partially off a very long, slender box, sitting nearby, and to his terror and amazement he beheld protruding from the box the feet of a woman. He did not stop to investigate, nor did he hesitate to talk, and soon the whole town and countryside were discussing with bated breath the gruesome discovery in Fox's drug store.

Fox was arrested, and tried in Chariton county on a charge of "body snatching," the fact having developed that the body was that of a young woman who had then but recently died in that county a few miles south of Marceline. The doctor's assistant, a man of excellent standing in the community, told the whole story on the witness stand, of a midnight ride in a buggy to the lonely cemetery; of the opening of the grave, over which the earth was yet new; of the return to town with the body between them in the buggy, and though there was no conviction in the case, it resulted in a radical change of the laws of the state of Missouri, so that now the hazard is too great, the penalty too severe for adventures of that kind and character.

After his arrest, Fox was bailed out for $3,000, and the desecrated body of the young woman, Leona Gates, was returned to the Bell Cemetery near Westville. Later developments in the story suggested that Fox and his assistant had been in the business of body-snatching for money. The trunk that had held Gates' corpse bore labels showing that it had passed through the Kansas City Union Depot as baggage no less than 17 times. Of course, it is unclear if Walt Disney knew of these events when he lived in Marceline, but one can certainly imagine them becoming Frankensteinian ghost story fodder among the town's children.

Thankfully, not all druggists in Marceline had run-ins with cadavers. In 1912, the drugstore of E. W. Tayler was the oldest continuously operating business in Marceline, and Tayler was considered to be the leading druggist in town. Brought up on a family farm, he had assumed ownership of his father's general store in 1901, after working there while studying pharmacy. Tayler was an active member of the community, belonging to the local school board, the Santa Fe Country Club Association, and the Masonic Order. The *Compendium* notes, "The people of Linn county esteem [Tayler] highly as a citizen and as a man, and he has a very considerable and helpful influence among them."

Likewise, in 1888, pharmacist Alonzo Withers established a drugstore in Marceline, beginning a successful career serving its residents.[53] He too was a farmer, and he had previously spent 10 years as a schoolteacher. As time went on, he purchased a second drugstore, an apothecary shop that *National Druggist* described as "old and well established… enjoying a good patronage." Two years later, he found a business partner and created the firm Withers & Blincoe. His leadership in the Marceline community continued throughout the Disney family's residence there.

Marceline was home to a number of other doctors and druggists as well, but there were two in particular who made significant impacts on young Walt Disney.

The first was Dr. William A. Cater. One of Marceline's earliest physicians, Cater owned a drugstore, though ironically, this is not where the influence on Disney came from. On the contrary, in addition to his medical practice, Dr. Cater was the manager of the Cater Opera House, which hosted road shows, vaudeville acts, and motion pictures. It was in the doctor's theatre that Walt Disney saw his first movies and a live performance of *Peter Pan*.

The other important figure was Doc Sherwood, a retired physician who lived close to the Disneys. He and his wife had no children, but they spent a great deal of time with young Walt, who became a sort of surrogate son to them. Sherwood owned a horse named Rupert, and when Walt drew a picture of the animal one day, Sherwood paid him a nickel for it. Dave Smith, the former director of The Walt Disney Archives, said of this event, "[This] was really Walt Disney's very first sale in the art field." Walt's brother Roy would later call it "the highlight of Walt's life."

It was with Doc Sherwood that Disney had some of his first exposure to pharmacies. Author Neal Gabler writes, "Walt often accompanied [Sherwood], even into the drugstore, where the doctor conducted a 'gabfest.' Usually on their trips Walt peppered him with questions, and years later he marveled at the doctor's knowledge and patience."

By 1910, Walt's father Elias had fallen into poor health, which led the family to sell their farm. Elias is believed to have had typhoid fever followed by pneumonia, so presumably, it was individuals like Tayler and Cater who cared for him from 1910 until 1911, when the family relocated to Kansas City, Missouri.

Shortly after their move, Elias purchased a paper route and put Walt to work doing deliveries. While he paid the other delivery boys a few dollars per week, Walt recalled, "He said that it was part of my job. I was part of the family. He said, 'I clothe and feed you.'... So he wouldn't pay me." As a result, Walt gained more exposure to the pharmacy field—unbeknownst to his father, he began making money delivering medicines for a drugstore while on his paper route.

As it happened, it was in a Kansas City drugstore that Walt first met his future sister-in-law Edna. She recalled that around 1911, "Roy and I were just going together... We stopped at a drugstore to get a soda, and Walt came to see Roy because he wanted a quarter or a half-dollar for paper to draw on."

Walt lived in Kansas City at a time when its local drugstores were experiencing significant growth. This is perhaps unsurprising since the city already had some 300,000 inhabitants, but in the span of just 30 years (1878-1908), the number of pharmacies in Kansas City had grown from just 22 to more than 300.[54]

Beyond simple urbanization and population growth, there were other factors that likely influenced this change. For one thing, in 1900, a law was passed in Missouri that helped to distinguish the professions of pharmacist and physician. Doctors in the 19th century often dispensed medications themselves, which greatly cut into the potential clientele of pharmacies. This new law took away physicians' ability to register as pharmacists unless they, too, passed the standard entrance exam.[55]

For another thing, Missouri's requirements for pharmacy licensure were very minimal. As mentioned previously, it was not until 1929 that druggists needed to have a college degree. Prior to this, the only requirements for registration in Missouri were:

- Four years' experience in a retail drugstore
- Two years' experience as an assistant pharmacist
- Must be at least 21 years of age
- Must demonstrate "good moral character"

Three years after Walt and his family moved to Kansas City, the Katz Drug Company was founded there. What began as a pair of humble cigar stores quickly grew, almost by accident, into one of the most profitable pharmacy chains in the world, an exemplar of the then-modern drug retailer. Over time, the company expanded to a nearly unheard-of 65 locations in five states. That same year, local druggist William Federmann incorporated four of his own drugstores to the tune of a quarter-million dollars.

Given that Walt himself was struggling to make ends meet at the time, one can imagine that the proprietors of drugstores like these—business owners enjoying self-made success—gave him something to aspire to.

Thus, even if Walt Disney did not realize it at the time, pharmacists and physicians played a significant role, both in his personal development and his development as a creator; one introduced him to the art of film, another validated his artistic ability and showed him that he could make money with it, and still others were businessmen and community leaders who Disney could look up to. They provided him with work, income, and encouragement. The Upjohn Pharmacy's very existence was, indirectly, a result of these experiences.

Though pharmacy was never a major theme in Disney's filmography, references to it did appear from time to time. One example is the 1934 Silly Symphony short entitled *The Wise Little Hen*. In this cartoon, the titular hen seeks the help of Donald Duck[56] and Peter Pig to plant and harvest corn for her babies for the winter. Too lazy to assist, Donald and Peter feign stomachaches, so the hen has to do all the work herself. When she realizes their scheme, she tricks the pair by making a large meal and seemingly preparing a basket of food to share with them. Inside the basket, however, Donald and Peter are disappointed to find not a delicious spread, but rather a bottle of foul-tasting castor oil, a common remedy of the time.

In an unusual coincidence, The Upjohn Company had opened a branch office in Kansas City in 1909, just two years before the Disneys arrived there. Located at 725 Wyandotte Street, the building was less than five miles from the Disneys' house on Bellefontaine Avenue.[57] Given its close proximity, it is reasonable to assume that Walt would have known the place. When considering his second residency in Kansas City (1919-1923), all doubt is removed; it is certain that he not only knew of the Upjohn office, but that he saw it regularly.

In 1918, around the time Walt was serving overseas in the American Ambulance Corps, the Kansas City Upjohn office moved from Wyandotte Street to a vacant plant at 25 East Pershing Road, the former home of a liquor wholesaler. The following year, Walt moved back to the city and began his animation career. His first paid cartooning job was at the Pesmen-Rubin Commercial Art Studio, just over a mile from the relocated Upjohn building.

Author Ron Green has documented many of the places where Walt Disney worked during his time in Kansas City. Below is a list of the specific locations Green cites and their approximate distances from the Upjohn office (all are within two miles):

- Pesmen-Rubin Commercial Art Studio
    - 14th and Oak streets (within the Gray Advertising Company)—*1.2 miles*
- Iwerks-Disney Studio
    - 13th and Oak streets (an unused bathroom in the headquarters of the National Restaurant Association)—*1.3 miles*
    - 7th and Walnut streets (Railway Exchange Building)—*1.6 miles*
- KayCee Studio
    - 30th and Holmes streets (a room above the Kansas City streetcar barn)—*1.2 miles*
    - 3239 Troost Avenue (second-floor office above the Standard Phonograph Company)—*1.9 miles*
- Laugh-O-Gram Films, Inc.
    - 1127 East 31st Street (second-floor studio in the McConahy Building)—*1.7 miles*
    - 3241 Troost Avenue (studio above Peiser's Restaurant)—*1.9 miles*

The relocated Upjohn building was squarely in the heart of town, just across the street from the new Kansas City Union Station. As Laugh-O-Gram Films faced bankruptcy in 1923, Disney was relegated to sleeping in his studio, with bread and canned beans for sustenance. "Once a week," writes Green, "he would pay a dime to take a bath at Union Station."

When Upjohn arrived in Kansas City, it too was struggling financially. During what has been called its "lean years," the company opened two new offices (the other being in San

Francisco), but due to poor accounting, it faced a fiscal challenge that threatened its continued existence. To make matters worse, with the advent of compressed tablet dosages in 1891, the friable pills that had kick-started the company were quickly falling out of favor with physicians. Upjohn faced declining sales, and its future looked grim.

Despite a prosperous beginning, by the turn of the century, founder W. E. Upjohn was taking out bank loans just to keep his company afloat. L. N. Upjohn, a later president of the company, once said he believed these to have been "character loans" based largely on W. E.'s respected position in the community. Much like Walt Disney's early fledgling endeavors, turn-of-the-century Upjohn found itself struggling just to get by.[58]

Though Walt Disney probably never had any business visiting the Kansas City Upjohn office, its mere presence there, just a stone's throw from his home and work, undoubtedly helped to establish brand identity in his mind. It is easy to imagine him, much later in life, regaling Donald Gilmore and Jack Gauntlett with stories of riding by the office on his bicycle or passing it on his way home from bathing at the train station.

Upjohn Health Films

"The health of man is like an equilateral...triiii-angle, completely dependent on the length and strength of each...siiiiiiide!" (Jingle from Upjohn's Triangle of Health films)

The connection between Disney and Upjohn extended beyond just the Upjohn Pharmacy. In the late 1960s, Upjohn spent $1.3 million to have Disney produce the Triangle of Health series, a collection of educational films about health topics. The four films produced for Upjohn were entitled:

- *Understanding Stresses and Strains* (1968)
- *Steps Toward Maturity and Health* (1968)
- *The Social Side of Health* (1969)
- *Physical Fitness and Good Health* (1969)

These films were animated shorts, occasionally interspersed with bits of live-action footage. Their target audience was families and school groups, so they featured cheerful animation[59] and catchy original songs. The films' credits included high-profile Disney creators, many of whom would later be named Disney Legends such as Les Clark, Eric Larson, and Hamilton Luske.[60]

Each installment was about 11 minutes long, and they centered around the notion of the titular equilateral triangle. This "Triangle of Health" represented the contemporary idea of the health of man, consisting of a physical side, a mental side, and a social side.

This tripartite view was likely based on the definition of health as put forth in the constitution of the World Health Organization in 1946. The first article of its preamble reads, "Health is a state of complete physical, mental and social well-being and not merely the absence of disease or infirmity." Though this definition does not conceptualize health in terms of an actual, literal triangle, it seems to have been adopted as such for ease of understanding.

The central theme throughout the Triangle of Health series was the importance of balance, and how the shape would become unstable if its sides were not in tune with one another.

Very little has been written about these films, but author Bob Cruz Jr. suggests that they were Disney's way of acknowledging "the new social climate" (i.e., the drug culture) of the late 1960s. However, he provides no substantive evidence to support this theory, and his rationale seems to be largely based on the fact that *Alice in Wonderland*, with its hookah-smoking caterpillar and size-changing mushrooms, had become popular with the counterculture.

While *The Social Side of Health* does indeed touch on the dangers of drug usage (even briefly depicting an acid trip!), it is merely a single topic within a larger lesson about social interactions. The entire drug sequence accounts for less than one minute of screen time in one film.

Cruz Jr. fails to consider the other three Upjohn films in the series—and even the rest of *The Social Side of Health*—which deal with entirely separate topics like stress management and fitness. (He also incorrectly lists one of the Triangle's sides as emotional, rather than mental.)

Contrary to Cruz Jr.'s assertions, Upjohn leveraged the Triangle of Health films as both educational PSAs and marketing tools. They were an extension of the Upjohn Pharmacy's marketing message, a way to reinforce the company's brand identity to families outside the gates of Disneyland. Case in point: In an internal letter about the films, Upjohn discussed the need for a "parallel program of advertising to tell [viewers] about The Upjohn Company, its goals and objectives, and its products." The letter also mentioned sponsoring a television broadcast of the films, with advertising, in conjunction with Disney's Sunday evening program. Just as the inclusion of "The Cell" model in Disneyland had done previously, the Triangle of Health films served to position Upjohn as a company devoted to scientific knowledge and community empowerment.

Produced over two and a half years, the Upjohn films were a significant part of Disney's venture into media production for outside industries. The July 1967 issue of *The Disney World* said of the project:

> This is by far the biggest step taken by the [Disney] Studio in the area of industrial films... The Upjohn series differs [from previous industrial media projects] in that the sponsor is interested only in institutional advertising values and is leaving everything to Disney, including the line of approach and the makeup of story material.

Prior to the *Triangle of Health* series, Disney had produced two other industrial films: *The Restless Sea* for AT&T and *Steel and America* for the American Iron & Steel Institute. Ken Peterson, the producer for the Upjohn series, said that these earlier projects had prepared Disney to tackle the Upjohn films: "The new series is going to be the best thing we have hit on so far and is what we have been aiming for all along—an industrial film program that will have really long-term values, to the company and its employees." He added, "The series will be, as Walt liked to put it, 'motivational.' It will not endeavor to teach or preach but rather to get all who see it to take action and, more important, to learn more about good health practices."[61]

The Upjohn Company had to be strategic in branding the films. Given that their intended demographic was primarily children, the company had to be sure that its messaging would be heard and understood, even by young viewers with no prior knowledge of Upjohn. Thus, each installment of the series opened and closed with sponsorship messages. The introductory bumper usually said:

> "A presentation on health by The Upjohn Company, makers of fine medicines through creative research."

Each episode then closed with:

> "This film is part of a continuing program by The Upjohn Company, in the interest of a better understanding of health."

Given that the average child likely knew very little about the pharmaceutical industry, these brief messages would have served to create an association between Upjohn and good health, thereby establishing brand recognition in a young audience. The content of the films was not exclusively child-focused, however. In particular, *Understanding Stresses and Strains* played to an older audience, and for this reason, it may be considered the most interesting of the entire Upjohn series. With an adult man as its main character, it discussed topics like the stresses of employment, and featured an extremely memorable song whose lyrics read:

Push, push
Rush, rush
Drive, drive
Go (x2)

Start your day with mounting tension
Watch the clock with apprehension
Off your seat
On your feet
Have to hurry up and meet
Stresses and strains!

To maintain your social status
Buy a status apparatus

Bigger car
There you are
Show 'em how you're going far
Stresses and strains!

Never mind your ills
Tranquilize with pills
Get yourself an ulcer over worry
Over bills

Take a few belts
Smoke up a storm
Be an individual
But try to conform

Don't lose sight of your ambition
Get ahead of competition
Be obsessed
Be the best
Haven't any time to rest

Something's breathing down your neck
It takes a great deal of pains
And lots of stresses and strains
To make a perrr-fect nerrrr-vous... wreck!

Author Ayesha Nathoo writes that *Understanding Stresses and Strains* was "firmly grounded in the contemporary reality of a Western metropolis." The film explored the question of how to remain healthy in a chaotic world filled with a constant barrage of stressors. She notes that it was regularly used as a lighthearted but effective teaching tool in relaxation classes, which, in addition to other psychosomatic therapies, had gained considerable popularity in the decades prior.

Unsurprisingly, the global drug industry reflected this changing of times. In the 1960s, hundreds of millions of prescriptions were written annually for psychotropic drugs such as tranquilizers, antidepressants, and sedatives. In 1963, Valium was brought to market, and it quickly became the most successful drug in history, a title it held until Prozac was introduced in the 1990s.

After the first four Triangle of Health films were completed, the series was put on hiatus for a decade, during which the relationship between Disney and Upjohn ended. Then, in 1979, Disney produced another film, this time under its own imprint, Walt Disney Educational Media Company. Entitled

Understanding Alcohol Use and Abuse,[62] this film bore similarities to the first four, but was decidedly darker in tone, depicting a drunk-driving accident and the silhouette of a man passed out against a dramatic red background. Though it reused the catchy jingle from the previous films, it also added a new title theme that could have easily come from *Halloween* or *The Exorcist*.

This attempted reboot of the series seemingly gained no traction, however, and the project was once again shelved, this time for more than a decade. Then, in late 1992, Disney released four more Triangle of Health films—this time live action—entitled *Keeping the Balance, Moving On, Personal Challenge,* and *True Friends.* The author has been unable to locate footage or substantive information about these films beyond brief summaries online, but there is likely little relevant information anyway since they had no affiliation with Upjohn.

Closure/Collection Movement

"Those old days were fun. The people working in all areas were pretty close; but, of course, the operation was not nearly as big as it is now. I left there more than 20 years ago, and I still occasionally run into people I knew and who remember me. It always brings back good memories." (Quote from Phil Harvey)

The Upjohn Company announced in 1970 that its Disneyland pharmacy would be closing its doors. A representative from Disneyland's sales division expressed regret, saying, "We, in the Disney organization, hate to see our long association end."

On September 23, 1970, the company hosted a farewell dinner in honor of the store's employees, and four days later, the store formally ceased operation.[63] After 15 years promoting its brand to Disneyland visitors, The Upjohn Company felt that the store had served its purpose.

Three main factors contributed to the Upjohn Pharmacy's closure. First, the connection between the Disney and Upjohn companies was built on the friendship of Walt Disney and Donald Gilmore. When Disney died in 1966, this foundational relationship was lost.[64] Second, by 1970, the Disney organization no longer lacked retail experience. Years of remarkable success had demonstrated that the park's shops provided steady revenue, and Disney had become confident that it could run them without the help of outside sponsors. Thus, as leases began to expire on Main Street, U.S.A., many were not renewed. Third, as the years had gone on, The Upjohn Company itself had experienced enormous growth and had come to view its Disneyland store as more of an expense than an investment. Put simply, times had changed and so had the company's priorities. What had begun as a basement business in the 19th century had grown into a global powerhouse with thousands of employees, an ever-growing list of subsidiaries, and presences in more than 50 cities around the world. At the time of the Upjohn Pharmacy's closure, a company spokesman said, "[I]t just isn't a judicious expenditure anymore."

The bulk of the Upjohn Pharmacy's collection was initially given to the California Museum of Science and Industry (today, called the California Science Center, and hereafter referred to as "CSC"). At the time, the value of the collection was estimated to be $35,000, but a letter attached to its inventory list noted that this figure may be on the high side. It read, "It just depends on who wants [the items], how badly they want them and how much money they have."

An internal CSC memo indicates that the museum planned to eventually display the collection in a projected community health building, but this exhibit never came to fruition. As a result, it is believed that the Upjohn collection was never actually displayed at CSC. In early 2008, CSC gave much of the collection to the History of Pharmacy Museum at the University of Arizona College of Pharmacy, where it resides today.

In November 2014, the author of this book completed work on an exhibit showcasing many of the artifacts from the Upjohn Pharmacy. Part of this installation featured a replica of the store's backsplash, decorated with its original materials. Archival photographs and documents were used to ensure accuracy, but the original design was expanded upon to maximize exhibit space. Then, in 2021, the collection was moved to a brand-new wing of the museum.[65] Thanks to generous donor support, this permanent installation finally gave the Upjohn collection the royal treatment it so deserved.[66]

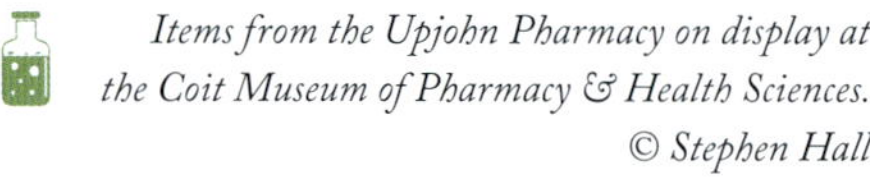

Items from the Upjohn Pharmacy on display at the Coit Museum of Pharmacy & Health Sciences.
© Stephen Hall

Tinct.
Quassiæ
Liq.
Amon.caust
Tinct.
Myrrhae
CASTOREI

While the majority of the Upjohn Pharmacy's items are in the care of the pharmacy museum today, a number are not. The whereabouts of some missing items are known, but others remain a mystery. Specifically, it is known that CSC disposed of bottles containing liquids in the early 1970s because of health concerns caused by leakage. Moreover, at least one item—the aforementioned mortar-and-pestle-shaped lamp—remains in Disney's possession. In 2015, it was displayed in an exhibit celebrating Disneyland's 60th anniversary. Since the pharmacy museum does not have the original piece, a detailed replica of the lamp was made for its Upjohn Pharmacy exhibit.

It is likewise known that many of the store's show globes belonged to manager Leo Austin, and they were returned to him when it closed. He kept the most valuable ones in his home and displayed the others in Upjohn's Los Angeles branch office. The antique microscopes, similarly, were returned to the company's headquarters in Michigan; an internal memo noted that they would be going into an exhibit there.[67]

The Upjohn Pharmacy's mortar-and-pestle-shaped lamp illuminated at night. © Coit Museum of Pharmacy & Health Sciences, The University of Arizona College of Pharmacy (used with permission)

Apothecary jars/bottles and antique microscopes on display in the Upjohn Pharmacy. © The Upjohn Company (used under fair use)

In addition to its antiques, CSC also received the pieces from the Upjohn Pharmacy's modern exhibit. Its plan was to display them in the would-be community health building and work with The Upjohn Company to keep them up to date. Disneyland purchased the Upjohn Pharmacy's casework for $2,500, and the proceeds went to CSC to fund backwalls, display cases, and other exhibit needs. W. G. Roberson, one of the Upjohn Pharmacy's later, full-time employees said of the new relationship with CSC:

> Frankly, we feel The Upjohn Company will be exposed to more people who are interested in such an exhibit... than was afforded by the Disneyland exposure. We can continue this association with the California Museum of Science and Industry at a cost of a few hundred dollars annually.

However, as of 2019, CSC's director of special exhibitions did not believe the museum still possessed these modern displays. Thus, their ultimate fate remains unclear.[68]

It is also unknown what became of the store's Wolf stove and herb grinder, among several other items. Perhaps strangest of all, though a 1958 Disneyland publication and the 1970 inventory list both mention a dozen pendant lamps hanging from the store ceiling, only six are in the pharmacy museum's possession. The author has been unable to determine the whereabouts of the others.

At the time of the Upjohn Pharmacy's closure, it had a staff of three full-time and three part-time employees. Only one, Phil Harvey, had been there since the beginning. Leo Austin had retired at the end of 1959 after 50 years with Upjohn and Fred Ekstein had left in 1961 to return to work in a retail drugstore. Substantive information cannot be found about the later staff members, but it is known the other two full-time employees retired shortly after the store closed. Phil Harvey was only 46, so he was not eligible for retirement. According to an Upjohn memo:

> Every effort was made to locate another job opportunity for Phil within the parent company and/or subsidiaries. At the present time, we have not located such an opening to meet his individual talents. [We] believe he will be in retail pharmacy work.

Harvey's son confirmed this years later, adding that his father went on to work in a Kaiser hospital pharmacy and then for independent drugstores before retiring.

In late 2020, the author made contact with Fred Ekstein, who by that time was 97 years old and the only surviving member of the original Upjohn Pharmacy staff.[69] Unfortunately, Mr. Ekstein did not wish to converse. "That was a long time ago," he said over the phone. "I really don't have anything to say."

A few years earlier, historian David Koenig had interviewed Ekstein for his book *The 55'ers: The Pioneers Who Settled Disneyland.* In an email to the author, Koenig said, "Whereas Phil evidently adored his time at Disneyland, Fred did not. I think he found the whole thing rather silly." This likely explains why Ekstein left the Upjohn store after several years to return to a more traditional pharmacy job.

As for the store itself, it seems to have remained an apothecary shop for a short time after Upjohn's lease ended. Three months after the store closed, an article in the *Kalamazoo Gazette* said, "An old-time drug store still operates on old Upjohn location, but the Upjohn name is gone."[70] In January 1972, the space formerly occupied by the Upjohn Pharmacy reopened as the New Century Clock Shop, sponsored by Elgin. In 1986, Lorus became the sponsor, and the store was renamed New Century Timepieces. This store continued operation until its closure in July 2008. Three months later, the space was again reopened under its current name, the Fortuosity Shop. For many years after Upjohn left, a sign hung on Main Street, U.S.A., advertising "℞ Drugs" in its honor.

As an amusing side note, there is an ongoing rumor (one might even call it a Disney urban legend) that when the Upjohn Pharmacy closed, the store's leeches were dumped into one of the park's waterways. Like the best urban legends, multiple versions of the story exist[71]—most accounts say the leeches were discarded in the Rivers of America, a few say it was the Jungle Cruise lagoon—but the general narrative is that the leeches caused an infestation in the water. Apparently, in the 1970s, not long after Upjohn had left the park, leeches were indeed found in a Disneyland waterway and the water was indeed drained. Some say it was drained because of the leeches, others say the draining was routine maintenance that happened to uncover them. One account even posits that the whole thing was the revenge tactic of a disgruntled Upjohn employee who was upset about the store closing! The reader can draw their own conclusions. If nothing else, the story is good for a chuckle.

Legacy/Future

"Those early years were fun, and there was a certain spirit throughout the park." (Quote from Fred Ekstein)

Today, the only remaining references to the Upjohn Pharmacy in Disneyland are names written on a window of the building. Described by *Overflow* as "Ad. Director Gauntlett's private joke," one of the high, corner windows bears the names of some Upjohn employees who were instrumental in the creation of the pharmacy, specifically Donald Gilmore, E. G. Upjohn, Fred Allen, and C. V. Patterson (Upjohn's executive vice president).

For more than 60 years, the Upjohn names were spread over two windows rather than one, but in 2019, a new window was added to the Fortuosity Shop/Upjohn Pharmacy to honor Dave Smith, the late founder of The Walt Disney Archives. Smith's window replaced the Patterson/Allen window, and the Patterson and Allen names were moved to the Gilmore/Upjohn window (see images to right).

One of the high, corner windows of the Fortuosity Shop/Upjohn Pharmacy, as it appeared in 2018. © Stephen Hall

Top right: The other window, as it appeared in 2018. © Stephen Hall

Bottom Right: The Upjohn window as it appears today, with the four names consolidated. © Stephen Hall

Far right: The Dave Smith window, added in 2019. © Stephen Hall

After the store closed, The Upjohn Company remained a dominant force in the drug industry for another 25 years, its business increasingly focusing on New Age research. In August 1995, the company announced a $13 billion merger with Swedish firm Pharmacia AB, a move aimed at selling huge quantities of drugs to HMOs and other organizations that bought medications in bulk. As a result of this merger, the newly formed Pharmacia & Upjohn became the ninth-largest drug company in the world. Five years later, another merger took place, this time between Pharmacia & Upjohn and Monsanto, another early Disneyland sponsor (see Endnote 48), who in 1985 had entered the drug market with the acquisition of G. D. Searle & Co. This merger rebranded the company as simply Pharmacia, and in 2003, Pfizer purchased Pharmacia for $60 billion, further solidifying Pfizer's position as the industry's top dog.[72]

Upjohn's Building 41, now owned by Pfizer, 2021. © Stephen Hall

The author of this book had the privilege of being the caretaker of the Upjohn Pharmacy collection from 2012 until 2022. With help from fellow historians and community members with connections to the Disney and Upjohn companies, the collection's preservation became a passion project. Primary documents and firsthand accounts have been immensely helpful in piecing together the larger story, but further historical research is ongoing.

Unfortunately, much of the documentation pertaining to the Upjohn Pharmacy (and The Upjohn Company itself) has been lost to history. Multiple sources confirm that the company's records were crudely disseminated near the end of its life; some documents and photographs were given to Western Michigan University, some physical artifacts to the Kalamazoo Valley Museum, but many items were simply discarded or destroyed between the late 1990s and early 2000s. In an email to the author, former Upjohn employee Jeremy Winkworth recalled personally salvaging some of the last remaining Upjohn records, which had been stored in a Pfizer document retention warehouse. "At the eleventh hour," he said, "I grabbed everything."[73]

In 2015, Mr. Winkworth donated two sets of Ektachrome photo slides to the History of Pharmacy Museum. The first set, taken by famed photographer Leonard Nadel, beautifully depicts the interior and exterior of the Upjohn Pharmacy, circa September 1955. The second set (photographer unknown, possibly Jack Gauntlett?) contains the early research images taken of the three New York City apothecaries the store was based on. Both sets of slides were Upjohn's originals, and the images were used in the *Scope* magazine articles about the Upjohn Pharmacy. At the time of donation, the slides had all experienced severe deterioration and red-shifting, but the University of Arizona's Center for Creative Photography was able to digitally draw out much of their original color, preserving a stunning visual record.

Later that year, the author had the pleasure of meeting George and Linda MacLeod, the son and daughter-in-law of Dr. A. Garrard MacLeod. In a recorded interview, George shared his memories of the Upjohn Pharmacy, *Scope* magazine, Will Burtin, and his father. His recollections and insights provided invaluable knowledge about the collection, most notably the provenance of the store's pendant lamps, dating back more than a century. He even offered a personal anecdote about his brother's 1953 discovery of the lamps, dust-covered and forgotten in a Kalamazoo drugstore, and their resulting inclusion in Disneyland.

Left to right) Author Stephen Hall, George MacLeod, Linda MacLeod, and Richard Wiedhopf in front of the Upjohn Pharmacy exhibit at the History of Pharmacy Museum, 2015. © Stephen Hall

In late 2019, the author was contacted by the College of Pharmacy at the University of Illinois at Chicago (UIC), where staff members had found a chalk drawing of the Upjohn Pharmacy in the college's possession. The author confirmed it to be one of the original, unused concept sketches of the store, drawn by Disney's designers. UIC had no records of how, when, or from whom it had acquired the drawing, but prior to this, the author had been unable to determine the whereabouts of any of these works, so it was exciting for one to surface. At least seven concept sketches are known to have been made, and the author continues to search for the others.

Then, in 2021, the History of Pharmacy Museum acquired at auction a set of nine architectural drawings of the Upjohn Pharmacy from Disney's initial design. The drawings show fine details like architectural scrollwork, light fixtures, and molding. They are attributed to the team of Earle G. Kaltenbach, whose work under the direction of Hollywood art director Gabe Scognamillo played a large role in the design of Disneyland.

Original concept drawing of the Upjohn Pharmacy.
Credit: University of Illinois Chicago College of Pharmacy (used with permission)

Today, nods to pharmacy history can be found elsewhere in Disneyland, though not associated with Upjohn/Pfizer. The queuing line for the Jungle Cruise ride is decorated with prop drug bottles made to look like those from the time period the ride re-creates. While many of these bottles bear the names of pretend drug products, some are labeled for real-life compounds such as aspirin, calomel, and witch hazel. Likewise, the Snow White ride features a scene of the Evil Queen preparing her poison. In this scene, riders can see tincture bottles labeled for compounds like Quassia amara, a plant commonly known as bitter ash.

Left and above: Prop drug bottles decorate the queuing line for the Jungle Cruise ride in Disneyland.
© Stephen Hall

Since the Upjohn Pharmacy exhibit opened at the History of Pharmacy Museum, thousands of patrons have seen and enjoyed it, including many who remembered visiting the store decades earlier. In conversations with former Upjohn employees, the author learned that very few at the company had known what became of the collection after 1970. This makes sense, as there were only a handful of people—mostly company executives—involved in its relocation, and it was never displayed at CSC. One former employee told the author that he attends a monthly breakfast with old colleagues, and that for years, every time they would meet, someone would inevitably bring up the Upjohn Pharmacy and speculate about what might have become of its antiques. He said that upon his return home to Kalamazoo, he was excited to inform the others that he had solved "the Disneyland mystery."

The Upjohn Pharmacy is an unusual, often forgotten piece of the Disneyland story. It spoke to the changing landscape of the pharmacy industry in the mid-20th century. It broke new, dynamic ground in the field of drug advertising. It symbolized the drugstore as an integral part of small-town living, an icon of Americana. Above all, it celebrated pharmacy's colorful history as it looked ahead to its exciting future. Though long gone from Main Street, U.S.A., the Upjohn Pharmacy leaves behind a legacy, and its story deserves to be told.

Author Stephen Hall at the Fortuosity Shop in Disneyland (formerly the Upjohn Pharmacy), 2015. © Stephen Hall

Special Thanks

Special thanks to Jeremy Winkworth (www.upjohn.net) *for his friendship, generosity, and continued willingness to assist me in my research. Thanks also to Luke Fernandez and the California Science Center* (www.californiasciencecenter.org), *Jay Follis, Emily Wiegand, and the Gilmore Car Museum* (www.gilmorecarmuseum.org), *Joseph Rheaume and the Center for Creative Photography* (www.creativephotography.org), *Dale Rush and the University of Illinois Chicago College of Pharmacy* (www.pharmacy.uic.edu), *Lynn Houghton, Christopher Tremblay, and the Western Michigan University Archives* (www.wmich.edu/library/archive-collections), *Brittany Williams, Regina Gorham, and the Kalamazoo Valley Museum* (www.kalamazoomuseum.org), *Greg Bond, Greg Higby, and the American Institute for the History of Pharmacy* (www.aihp.org), *Mark and Beth Ballard* (www.disneyhistory101.com), *Marcy Smothers* (www.foodwinemarcy.com), *Kaye Malins and the Walt Disney Hometown Museum* (www.waltdisneymuseum.org), *Michael Wells and the Kansas City Public Library* (www.kclibrary.org), *Alex Merrill and the Kalamazoo Public Library* (www.kpl.gov), *my brother Philip Hall, my parents John and Jean Hall, Metta Lou Henderson, Richard Wiedhopf, Michael Virgintino, Toba Hartmann, Kevin Kern, Didier Ghez, Brad Abbott, James Keeline, David Koenig, Mary Becktell, Phil Carra, Don Parfet, Peter Seaver, Elizabeth Yarger, Steve Cookson, Virgil Williams, and George and Linda MacLeod.*

Author Stephen Hall in the Upjohn Pharmacy exhibit at the Coit Museum of Pharmacy & Health Sciences, 2022. © Stephen Hall

Endnotes

1 Reference 134 incorrectly states that Gilmore's and Disney's winter residences were in Arizona.

2 According to the Gilmore Car Museum and Disney's archivists, this set piece—an oversized replica of the Rolls-Royce's backseat—is believed to be the only set piece to ever leave Disney studios' possession.

3 The Gilmores also sponsored the development of the Gilmore Art Center at the Kalamazoo Institute of Arts. They made a deal with Walt Disney that they would donate money to the Chouinard Art Institute in Los Angeles if he in turn would donate money to the Kalamazoo Institute.

4 For about eight years, Jack Gauntlett was a part of the Upjohn family by marriage. He was the first husband of Barbara Upjohn DeLano, a descendant of W. E. Upjohn.

5 Ironically, Gilmore may have passed on an earlier chance to invest in Disneyland; author Marcy Smothers writes that Disney had extended the opportunity to fellow Smoke Tree Ranch residents, colloquially known as "Colonists," but all of them had declined.

6 The author interviewed numerous retired Upjohn employees and associates while writing this book, all of whom were full of warm memories and amusing anecdotes like this. One employee recalled the company's barbershop and how Donald Gilmore would say, "If your hair grows on company time, we'll cut it on company time." Another reminisced about the spectacular rhubarb pie served in the company cafeteria and how residents from the Kalamazoo community would dine there before security was a concern. Still another spoke of the company's softball team and the specially made bottles of vanilla that were only available to employees. In each case, the individual expressed utmost pride for having worked at Upjohn.

7 Interestingly, Upjohn was not the only Kalamazoo-based company involved with early Disneyland. In 1957, the Kalamazoo Manufacturing Company produced a replica of an old-time railroad handcar, specially made to fit the "narrow-gauge 30-inch tracks" in Disneyland.

8 The original Ektachrome slides of these images, and others from the Upjohn Pharmacy, are in the archives of the University of Arizona's Coit Museum of Pharmacy & Health Sciences.

9 Shortly before Disneyland's opening, noted pharmacy historian George Griffenhagen wrote that the Upjohn store would be "based on specifications from three operating drugstores which have changed very little since 1890." Gauntlett made a similar statement around the same time, but he took it further, saying the stores had changed very little in 150 years. This was indeed true for the Olliffe apothecary, which was exactly 150 years old, but the Cassebeer apothecary was only 112 years old and the Lascoff apothecary only 56.

10 The author believes this to have been the residence of Frances Elizabeth "Fannie" Barrett, one of W. E. Upjohn's nieces and an Upjohn family historian.

11 Under Burtin's direction, Upjohn's branding was changed from the old-time visage of a pill under founder W. E. Upjohn's thumb to the text-only logo that would last the rest of the company's life. An Upjohn spokesman once described the appeal of Burtin's work, calling it "highly progressive in concept but couched in an idiom that partook of the scientific in its clarity and definiteness."

12 Upjohn was not the only pharmaceutical company for which Burtin did work. Two years before Disneyland opened, he also developed product branding for Ecuadoran drugmaker Life Farmacéuticos.

13 The actual numbers were slightly less; annual attendance did not surpass six million until the 1960s.

14 Trahan et al. note that E. G. Upjohn was president of the National Vitamin Foundation and suggest this as a possible reason for Unicap's distribution in Disneyland.

15 Detail men can be thought of as the predecessors of modern drug reps.

16 The paintings mentioned here are easily the most notable of all these practitioner-focused promotions. Between 1948 and 1964, Parke, Davis & Company sponsored the creation of two fabulous painting series, entitled ***Great Moments in Pharmacy*** and ***Great Moments in Medicine***. These two series, with a combined total of 85 images, were the result of a collaboration between artist Robert Thom and historian George Bender, who was the company's advertising director. The pair traveled the world, visiting countless historical sites and consulting with subject-matter experts. The resulting works gained international acclaim—particularly the pharmacy series—and prints were distributed far and wide. When George Bender retired in 1969, he moved to Tucson, Arizona, and began teaching a history course at the University of Arizona College of Pharmacy. By coincidence, while he was there, he also served as curator of the History of Pharmacy Museum, a role the author of this book would hold 40 years later. Today, the ***Great Moments in Pharmacy*** paintings belong to the American Pharmaceutical Association and the ***Great Moments in Medicine*** paintings belong to the University of Michigan. All of Bender's original notes and research reside in the archives of the Coit Museum of Pharmacy & Health Sciences. (Interestingly, they include information about a would-be ***Great Moments in Nursing*** series that was never made.) In 2021, with the unveiling of an all-new wing, the museum opened an interactive exhibit in which the pharmacy paintings are brought to life using parallax animation.

17 However, ***Drug Topics*** noted in August 1955 that, though no merchandise was sold in the apothecary area, out of the store's modern exhibit space, "a limited number of items [were] sold for the convenience of visitors to Disneyland." The author has been unable to determine what these items were and has not seen any other mentions of them.

18 According to the pamphlet that was given to Upjohn Pharmacy visitors, this lamp originally decorated a drugstore in Philadelphia, but was acquired in Charleston along with over 100 other items. The piece originally bore the name of the Philadelphia store's proprietor (likely Morgan) but was modified to bear the Upjohn name.

19 These fabulous majolica vats are something of a mystery. Despite their size—each one is over 3 feet tall and almost 2 feet in diameter—incredibly few pictures exist that show them on display. Upjohn's press photographs were taken in 1955, and the fact that none of them show these vessels all but guarantees they were not there at the beginning. An inventory of the store from 1970 (Reference 56) lists them as having been displayed in the "Small Front Windows," and image on page 43, dated 1962, confirms this to be the case. Still, it is unclear exactly how, where, or from whom they were acquired, or when, prior to August 1962, they were added to the store. Regardless, these pieces are arguably the finest items in the entire Upjohn Pharmacy collection.

20 One estimate dated these lamps to the 1860s, another to the 1890s.

21 The Upjohn family's history is astoundingly well documented in Light 1990 (Reference 74), dating back as far as the early 16th century. Ancestors from the family's pre-pharmaceutical days included clockmakers, carpenters, and architects, just to name a few.

22 During the 1870s alone, seven Upjohns studied medicine at the University of Michigan and two studied pharmacy. Many more would pursue health science degrees later, including dentistry and nursing. Of Uriah's children, it was not only the males who went to college, either. His oldest child, Helen, was in the Michigan medical school class of 1872, a time when female doctors were woefully few.

23 W. E. and his siblings had grown up on a farm, where they frequently had to repair and/or improvise equipment. His brother Henry devised a feed cutter, a cultivator, and a knot-tying device for hay-binding machines. W. E. himself followed the Upjohn family tradition by tinkering with clocks at a young age.

24 Historically, the term "pill" was used to describe a specific kind of dosage, distinct from a tablet, capsule, etc. Pills were typically spherical in shape and formed by hand using a pill roller. Soon after the introduction of the tablet press, which was far more accurate and efficient than any dosage-making technology before it, pills were rendered obsolete.

25 Parke, Davis & Company was the other notable drugmaker in Michigan. Founded 20 years prior to Upjohn, this Detroit-based manufacturer made countless major contributions to the industry. In time, both companies would come to be owned by Pfizer.

26 In a not-so-subtle dig at competitors, Upjohn ran an ad in 1896 with the tagline "under the thumb versus under the hammer," implying that rival pills were so rigid they would need a hammer to crush.

27 The image of a pill under Dr. Upjohn's thumb would quickly become iconic and would remain the company's logo for decades. It has been called the most famous thumb in history.

28 The name was changed to "The Upjohn Company" in 1902.

29 In Arizona, which was still a territory at the time, the barrier to entry was essentially nonexistent. The first territorial pharmacy law would not even be passed until 1903. Prior to that, as pioneer druggist Andrew Martin recalled, "anyone could call himself a pharmacist by simply painting a sign in front of his place of business reading 'Blank's Drug Store.' He could fill prescriptions, sell narcotics, and treat the sick without restraint."

30 The connection between photography and pharmacy continues to this day. Though film photography is largely a thing of the past, most chain drugstores still have a photo counter!

31 Despite their ubiquity, the Upjohn Pharmacy did not actually have a soda fountain. The reason for this is clear, however: there was one nearby at the Carnation ice cream parlor.

32 Disney Studios' Animation Coffee Shop and Penthouse Club also featured dining counters designed with a classic American drugstore look.

33 W. E.'s involvement in the Kalamazoo community was extensive and impactful, so much so that he would come to be called the city's "First Citizen." Aside from his work at The Upjohn Company, he helped to establish churches and a local hospital, donated land for numerous civic projects, and even served as the mayor of Kalamazoo!

34 The western U.S. had no pharmacy schools until 1872, when the California College of Pharmacy opened (only the 10th such school in the country). In neighboring Arizona, the first college of pharmacy would not be established until 1947.

35 Today, this organization is called the American Association of Colleges of Pharmacy.

36 As a historical side note, pharmacy students before 1929 did not always receive a traditional B.S. degree. In 1907, a two-year Ph.G. (Graduate in Pharmacy) degree was set as the minimum national standard, and in 1925, the standard was increased to a three-year Ph.C. (Pharmaceutical Chemist) degree. Today, both of these are ancient, obscure history. The modern Pharm.D. (Doctor of Pharmacy) degree did not come about until 1950, and it did not become the national standard until many years after that.

37 Prohibition was a key factor in the rise of hospital pharmacy. Since alcohol was frequently prescribed to patients, hospital pharmacists were responsible for inventory control and the manufacture of alcohol-based preparations.

38 In 1937, the American Hospital Association produced a report outlining the need for hospital pharmacists. The report established guidelines, including a recommendation that any hospital with more than 100 beds should employ a pharmacist. It took some time for these guidelines to be widely adopted, however. Even into the late 1950s, less than 40 percent of hospitals had a full-time pharmacist.

39 Interestingly, Upjohn's wartime production was not just limited to medications—for a brief time, its machine shop was subcontracted to manufacture airplane parts!

40 When the Portage plant opened, it was several miles outside of town, which made it difficult for employees, especially those without cars, to commute. In 1949, Upjohn began operating a fleet of buses that shuttled employees to and from work. Sleekly painted in gray, black, and white, and bearing the destination sign "UPJOHN SPECIAL," these vehicles came to be known as the "Gray Ghosts."

41 Many reputable, ethical drug companies had run-ins with this law, including Upjohn itself. For years, Dr. W. E. Upjohn had considered venturing into the candy business, and in 1911, The Upjohn Company began selling so-called "Kazoo Mints." Shortly after the candy's debut, Upjohn was charged with food adulteration. As it turned out, no one at Upjohn had realized that starch, a common ingredient in drug manufacturing, was classified as an adulterant when used in candy molding.

42 Eventually, the American Medical Association drew a distinction between patent drugs and drugs listed in the *United States Pharmacopoeia*. The latter were given the classification "ethical."

43 In addition to various consumer safety regulations, this legislation also set rules for prescribing. Though 19th-century licensing laws had given physicians the authority to prescribe, prescriptions were not required until well into the 20th century. This meant that for decades, most any drug that could be acquired with a prescription could also be acquired without one. The reason was that the modern, two-tier system of over-the-counter versus prescription medications did not yet exist. Prior to 1938, there was no distinction between drugs that were to be used only under a doctor's supervision and drugs that patients could use to self-medicate.

44 This journal featurette states that the company was founded in 1885, not 1886. This could debatably be considered correct, since The Upjohn Pill and Granule Company technically became an official partnership in the fall of 1885, but according to the company's centennial history, "[B]ecause the earliest date in company records falls in [1886]—a handwritten notation on the first price list—1886 is considered the firm's date of birth." Both the sign inside and the lamp outside the Upjohn Pharmacy read "THE UPJOHN COMPANY—FOUNDED 1886."

45 This notion of "doctor as druggist" was not unique to the American West. Country doctors the nation over would travel great distances to care for patients. Uriah Upjohn himself sometimes rode 40 or more miles per day on horseback to bring quinine and other medications to the sick in Michigan!

46 Disney would visit Kalamazoo again in September 1964 on his way home from Washington, D.C., where he received the Presidential Medal of Freedom from Lyndon Johnson. During this second trip, which was more for pleasure than business, Disney visited numerous sites including the Upjohn headquarters, the Gilmore Brothers department store, the Kalamazoo Art Center, Gull Lake, and the site of the soon-to-be-established Gilmore Car Museum. Upjohn Pilot Virgil Williams shared with the author a memory of Disney's second visit, saying, "We had a call from Donald Gilmore here in Kalamazoo, and he wanted to know if we could put Walt Disney's Gulfstream I in our hangar for the weekend. We said, 'Absolutely!' Disney came into our hangar and the Gilmores met him there. In his airplane, all the leather headrests on the backs of the seats were engraved with the various Walt Disney characters—Donald Duck, Pluto, Mickey Mouse. Walt was very nice, very courteous." In honor of Disney's 1964 visit, and in conjunction with Western Michigan University's "Walt's Pilgrimage" course, the mayor of Kalamazoo in 2018 declared July 12 "Walt Disney Day."

47 At least three copies of "The Cell" were made, one larger- and two smaller-scale. It was one of the latter that was featured at Disneyland. These models traveled all over the world and were exhibited at various health science events, including the conventions of the American Medical and Veterinary Associations. In 1959, the larger, 24-foot model became a permanent exhibit at the Chicago Museum of Science and Industry, but it was removed and destroyed in 1967, "after it was determined that it had suffered too much wear and tear and was becoming obsolete scientifically." The author has been unable to conclusively determine the fate of the others.

48 The Upjohn Pharmacy was not the only place in Disneyland that featured larger-than-life scientific exhibits. For years, Tomorrowland was home to the Monsanto Hall of Chemistry, which stood roughly in the location of the Star Tours ride that followed. The Hall of Chemistry featured oversized exhibits like the "Chemitron," a display of gigantic test tubes representing the eight natural materials—salt, coal, air, oil, sulfur, phosphate rock, water, and limestone—from which some 500 Monsanto products were made. The Hall remained in Disneyland from 1955 until 1966. After it closed, Monsanto kept a presence in the park, sponsoring the classic Adventure Thru Inner Space ride.

49 Disneyland also had a Welch's juice bar.

50 The timeline of Schering's development is a bit complex, and there were several notable dates involved. Like many 19th-century drug companies, Schering grew out of an apothecary shop, in this case that of Ernst Schering, which opened in 1851. 20 years later, the joint stock company Chemische Fabrik auf Actien (Vorm. E. Schering) was incorporated, and the actual corporate entity Schering AG followed in 1890. The Schering Corporation was established much later, on December 27, 1928.

51 For what it is worth, historian Christopher Kobrak notes that while Schering was indeed complicit in despicable wartime activities, the company seems to have been somewhat reticent in its involvement. He cites Schering's minimum compliance with the German government's mandates, but also notes that the company may have simply been looking out for its own long-term business interests.

52 The author would love to know what became of the Schering Apothecary's antiques after the store closed. He suspects they either remained in Schering's possession, perhaps being moved to a corporate office somewhere, or else that they were returned to Sydney Blumberg. If they were in fact returned, the author's next question would pertain to the whereabouts of Mr. Blumberg's collection today.

53 Withers' store opened one year after the Tayler general store, but since the latter was not originally a drugstore, this might mean that Withers was actually Marceline's first pharmacist.

54 In 1920, there were at least four drugstores within two blocks of the former Disney home on Bellefontaine Avenue, and dozens more nearby. The proprietors of the four closest stores were H. C. Dickey, C. R. Ryan, H. L. Rogers, and J. T. Bennett. These stores were likely in operation during the Disneys' residence in Kansas City (1911-1917), meaning young Walt probably frequented them and knew their owners.

55 Urdang and Kremers note that shortly before the law went into effect, 2,242 physicians registered as pharmacists, presumably so they could avoid taking the exam.

56 ***The Wise Little Hen*** was Donald Duck's first onscreen appearance.

57 As a side note, the Kansas City College of Pharmacy was located just a couple of doors down from the Upjohn office, at 712-714 Wyandotte Street.

58 Upjohn's saving grace came in 1908 with the introduction of Phenolax. These laxative wafers, which would later come to be known as "Dr. W. E.'s 'big thing,'" were a major success because they were the first pleasant-tasting laxative to come to market. In their first year of production, close to 20 million wafers were sold, followed by over 45 million in 1909, and over 100 million by 1914. The drug's popularity peaked in 1924 with sales of 182 million, but for decades thereafter, Phenolax remained a staple of the Upjohn catalog. Donald Gilmore would later refer to his Kalamazoo home, which was completed in 1925, as "the house Phenolax built."

59 Cruz Jr. accurately notes that the films' animation was of lower quality than typical Disney productions, comparing it to "the far-less-detailed work of rival studio Hanna-Barbera."

60 ***Understanding Stresses and Strains*** was the last film Luske worked on before his death.

61 Peterson also mentions the possibility of pamphlets and books being developed to supplement the films. The author has been unable to find any further information about these, including whether they were produced at all.

62 ***Understanding Alcohol Use and Abuse*** reuses the title characters from Disney's World War II short ***Reason and Emotion***. In both films, the human brain is controlled by a pair of goofy characters within. Reason, the archetypal "nerd" character, usually sits at the steering wheel of the brain, but occasionally, Emotion, the troublemaking caveman character, takes over, often with disastrous results. Interestingly, the 2015 Disney/Pixar hit ***Inside Out*** seems to borrow its premise from these films.

63 Reference 91, an Upjohn publication from the company's centennial, incorrectly lists the year of its closure as 1972.

64 Less than two months before his death, Disney wrote Gilmore a letter in which he mentioned he would be going to the hospital for a pinched nerve in his neck. An X-ray related to his procedure revealed that he had lung cancer. A few years after Disney died, Gilmore stepped down from his leadership position on Upjohn's board. He had served as chairman from 1953 until 1961, and then as vice chairman until 1969. After leaving the vice chairmanship, he

continued as a board member for another decade, finally retiring in January 1979. Gilmore died in December of that year, at age 84.

65 This new museum wing includes four distinct exhibit areas. The first is the Upjohn Pharmacy exhibit, featuring the store's antiques, and the adjoining, second exhibit deals with contemporary, 21st-century health science. This layout was designed intentionally to echo the "then and now" mentality of the Upjohn Pharmacy.

66 In recognition of this support, and in light of the museum expanding its focus to encompass both modern science and health disciplines beyond just pharmacy, the museum's name was also changed from the History of Pharmacy Museum to the Coit Museum of Pharmacy & Health Sciences.

67 Because these show globes and microscopes were never given to CSC, and therefore never made it to the History of Pharmacy Museum, it is unclear what ultimately became of them after Pharmacia and Upjohn merged in 1995. The Kalamazoo Valley Museum possesses one hanging globe that may have been displayed in Disneyland, but the others cannot be found. The author has reached out to multiple sources who have documentation and firsthand knowledge of The Upjohn Company and its closure, but none have any leads on these other items.

68 Since the rotating columns from the Upjohn Pharmacy's modern exhibit are likely lost to history, the Coit Museum had a photograph of them blown up into a large wall graphic. This graphic was placed in the museum's own modern exhibit, which adjoins its Upjohn Pharmacy display.

69 Leo Austin passed away in 1980, followed by Juanita Goodwin in 1992, Betty Lou Foley in 1996, and Phil Harvey in 2014.

70 The author suspects that the antiques were allowed to remain in Disneyland while the donation to CSC was being coordinated.

71 Mentions of this rumor can be found on numerous message boards across Disney fan-sites. The author also corresponded with several former cast members who shared their personal recollections of the story.

72 During the COVID-19 pandemic, Pfizer's vaccine was produced in two former Upjohn plants: the main one in Portage (primarily in Building 41) and another in Puurs, Belgium. The fact that these decades-old facilities could handle the production of such a globally important vaccine is a testament to how far The Upjohn Company was ahead of its time.

73 In 2007, Upjohn's corporate headquarters building was demolished after being deemed "useless." The razing of Building 88, which Kalamazoo residents had lovingly come to call the "Taj Mahal," seemed to symbolically mark the end of Upjohn.

References

1. "$1,300,000 Upjohn Series Demonstrates New Industry Needs." ***The Disney World***, July 1967.
2. "About." ***W. E. Upjohn Institute for Employment Research***, www.upjohn.org/about.
3. Adams, Samuel Hopkins. ***The Great American Fraud***. New York: P.F. Collier & Son, 1905. https://books.google.com/books/about/The_Great_American_Fraud.html?id=tdf8na3fqNUC.
4. Allen, David. "Disneyland: Another Kind of Reality." ***European Journal of American Culture*** 33, no. 1 (2014): 33-47. doi:10.1386/ejac.33.1.33_1.
5. "Annual Report of the Missouri Board of Pharmacy." Missouri Board of Pharmacy, 1920. https://hdl.handle.net/2027/mdp.39015068164980?urlappend=%3Bseq=57.
6. Ballentine, Carol. "Taste of Raspberries, Taste of Death: The 1937 Elixir Sulfanilamide Incident." ***FDA Consumer Magazine***, June 1981. https://www.fda.gov/files/about fda/published/The-Sulfanilamide-Disaster.pdf.
7. Barrier, Michael. ***The Animated Man: A Life of Walt Disney***. Berkeley, CA: University of California Press, 2007.
8. Barry, Pennan M., Alexander W. Kay, Jennifer M. Flood, and James Watt. "Getting to Zero: Tuberculosis Elimination in California." ***Current Epidemiology Reports*** 3, no. 2 (2016): 136-144. https://doi.org/10.1007/s40471-016-0076-6.
9. Baxter, John. ***Disney During World War II: How the Walt Disney Studio Contributed to Victory in the War***. New York: Disney Editions, 2014.
10. Bemis, Bethanee. "Mirror, Mirror for Us All: Disney Theme Parks and the Collective Memory of the American National Narrative." ***The Public Historian*** 42, no. 1 (2020): 54-79. https://doi.org/10.1525/tph.2020.42.1.54.
11. Bender, G. A. ***A History of Arizona Pharmacy***. Tucson, AZ: Arizona Pharmacy Historical Foundation, 1985.
12. Bingham, A. Walker. ***The Snake-Oil Syndrome: Patent Medicine Advertising***. Hanover, MA: Christopher Pub. House, 1994.
13. Bowdoin Van Riper, A. ***Learning from Mickey, Donald and Walt: Essays on Disney's Edutainment Films*** (essay by Bob Cruz Jr.). Jefferson, NC: McFarland & Co., 2011.
14. Broholm, Richard. "The Upjohn Company, 1884-1932." Paper from the History Seminar of Kalamazoo College, January 1950. http://upjohn.net/corporate/early/1950_history_seminar_broholm.pdf.
15. "Building a Small World." Bank of America, August 13, 2014. https://about.bankofamerica.com/en-us/our-story/building-a-small-world.html#fbid=4Cw-Bikcb3o.
16. Burnes, Brian, Dan Viets, and Robert W. Butler. ***Walt Disney's Missouri: The Roots of a Creative Genius***. Kansas City: Kansas City Star Books, 2002.
17. Cahn, Julius. ***Julius Cahn's Official Theatrical Guide, Volume XIV***. New York: Julius Cahn, 1909.
18. Carlisle, Robert D. B. ***A Century of Caring: The Upjohn Story***. Elmsford, NY: Benjamin, 1987.
19. Clark, Alfred E. "Donald S. Gilmore of Upjohn Company." ***The New York Times***, December 24, 1979. Accessed October 8, 2020. https://www.nytimes.com/1979/12/24/archives/donald-s-gilmore-of-upjohn-company-retired-chief-executive-played.html.
20. Clark, Peter M. to L. C. Hoff. June 01, 1970.
21. Clément, Thibaut. "'They All Trust Mickey Mouse': Showcasing American Capitalism in Disney Theme Parks." ***InMedia: The French Journal of Media Studies*** 7, no. 1 (2018). https://journals.openedition.org/inmedia/1021.
22. ***Compendium of History and Biography of Linn County, Missouri***. Chicago: Henry Taylor & Co., 1912.
23. "Dave Smith's New Window." Series of emails between Kevin Kern

(Walt Disney Archives) and author. January 2022.

24. Disney, Walt. July 17, 1955. Disneyland Dedication Speech, Disneyland, Anaheim, CA.
25. "Disney Exhibit Highlights Turn-Of-Century Store." ***Drug Topics***, August 22, 1955.
26. "Disney Health Films." W. H. Bayliss to R. T. Parfet. February 20, 1967, 138-139.
27. "'Disneyland' Drugstore Shows Pharmacy Progress." ***The Louisiana Pharmacist*** 14, no. 9 (1955): 6-7.
28. "Disneyland Store." W. C. Sugg to W. G. Roberson. September 27, 1961.
29. Donohue, Julie. "A History of Drug Advertising: The Evolving Roles of Consumers and Consumer Protection." ***The Milbank Quarterly*** 84, no. 4 (2006): 659-699.
30. Dumay, Jan. "The Enduring Legacy of Katz Drug Stores." ***Kansas City Magazine***, August 11, 2014. https://www.kansascitymag.com/the-enduring-legacy-of-katz-drug-stores/.
31. Earles, Melvin P. "Book Review: The Royal Apothecaries." ***Pharmacy in History*** 11, no. 1 (1969): 25.
32. "Edna Disney." D23: The Official Disney Fan Club. Accessed July 22, 2020. https://d23.com/walt-disney-legend/edna-disney/
33. Engel, Leonard. ***Medicine Makers of Kalamazoo***. New York: McGraw-Hill, 1961.
34. Fathelrahman, Ahmed Ibrahim, Mohamed Izham Mohamed Ibrahim, Alian A. Alrasheedy, and Albert I. Wertheimer. ***Pharmacy Education in the Twenty First Century and Beyond: Global Achievements and Challenges***. London: Academic Press, 2018.
35. "Final Status, Disneyland Pharmacy Closing." W. E. Glenn to L. C. Hoff. September 30, 1970.
36. Fjellman, Stephen. ***Vinyl Leaves: Walt Disney World and America***. Boulder: Westview Press, 1992.
37. Francaviglia, Richard. "History After Disney: The Significance of 'Imagineered' Historical Places" ***The Public Historian*** 17, no. 4 (Autumn 1995): 69-74.
38. Frank, Robert, and Scott Hensley. "Pfizer to Buy Pharmacia For $60 Billion in Stock." ***The Wall Street Journal***, July 15, 2002. Accessed May 2, 2021. https://www.wsj.com/articles/SB1026684057282753560.
39. "Freedomland Apothecary Shop." Series of emails between Mike Virgintino, Toba Hartmann, and author. July 2020.
40. Gabler, Neal. ***Walt Disney: The Triumph of the American Imagination***. New York: Knopf, 2006.
41. Getlen, Larry. "Freedomland Theme Park Was a '60s Apple Slice of Americana." ***New York Post***, February 21, 2019. https://nypost.com/2019/02/21/freedomland-theme-park-was-a-60s-apple-slice-of-americana/.
42. Gilmore, Donald S. "1953 in Summary." ***The Overflow***, March 1954.
43. Green, Ron. "The Roots of Animation in Kansas City." ***The Jackson County Historical Society Journal*** 52, no. 1 (2014): 15-19.
44. Greene, Jeremy A. "Attention to 'Details.'" ***Social Studies of Science*** 34, no. 2 (2004): 271-292. https://doi.org/10.1177/0306312704043029.
45. Griffenhagen, George B., and Gregory Higby. ***150 Years of Caring: A Pictorial History of the American Pharmaceutical Association***. Washington, D.C.: American Pharmaceutical Association, 2002.
46. Griffenhagen, George. "Collector's Corner." ***Journal of the American Pharmaceutical Association*** 16, no. 2 (May 1955): 276. doi: https://doi.org/10.1016/S0095-9561(16)33708-2.
47. https://www.facebook.com/groups/disneyhistoryinstitute/permalink/3411052078973358.
48. Hill, Gus. ***Gus Hill National Theatrical Directory***, 1914-1915. New York: Hill's National Theatrical Directory, Inc., 1914.
49. "History." UCSF School of Pharmacy. Accessed November 29, 2020. https://pharmacy.ucsf.edu/about/history/.
50. Holdford, David A. "Chapter 2: Overview of the History of Hospital Pharmacy in the United States." In ***Introduction to Acute & Ambulatory Care Pharmacy Practice***, 19-39. Bethesda, MD: ASHP Publications, 2017.
51. "Interoffice Memorandum: Refurbishing Disneyland." H. S. Cripe to John Deal. March 12, 1959.

52. Interview with Don Parfet, Peter Seaver, and Phil Carra, by author. August 18, 2021.
53. Interview with George MacLeod, by author. November 4, 2015.
54. Interview with Phil Carra, by author. May 26, 2021.
55. Interview with Virgil Williams, by author. December 14, 2020.
56. "Inventory of Disneyland Exhibit." W. G. Roberson to W. E. Glenn. June 23, 1970.
57. Ireton, Michelle. "Legendary architect Bruce J. Graham dies at age 84." MLive, March 13, 2010. Accessed April 30, 2021. https://www.mlive.com/news/kalamazoo/2010/03/legendary_architect_dies.html.
58. "It's Official: Pfizer Buys Pharmacia." CNNMoney. April 16, 2003. Accessed May 2, 2021. https://money.cnn.com/2003/04/16/news/companies/pfizer_pharma/.
59. Jackson, Kathy M., and Mark I. West. *Disneyland and Culture: Essays on the Parks and Their Influence.* Jefferson, NC: McFarland &, 2011.
60. Johnson, Kyleigh. "Walt Disney Archives Founder Dave Smith Honored with Window on Main Street, U.S.A., at Disneyland Park." Disney Parks Blog. The Walt Disney Company, January 24, 2022. https://disneyparks.disney.go.com/blog/2022/01/walt-disney-archives-founder-dave-smith-honored-with-window-on-main-street-u-s-a-at-disneyland-park/.
61. *Kalamazoo Art Center (1959-1965).* https://wou.edu/wp/exhibits/files/2015/07/Kalamazoo-Art.pdf.
62. "Kalamazoo Company Reproduces 'Gay Nineties' Handcar for Disneyland." *The Kalamazoo Gazette*, May 12, 1957.
63. King, Margaret J. "Disneyland and Walt Disney World: Traditional Values in Futuristic Form." *The Journal of Popular Culture* 15, no. 1 (1981): 129-30. doi:10.1111/j.0022-3840.1981.00116.x.
64. Kirby, Irwin. "Freedomland Opens With Huge Throng, Publicity Scores." *The Billboard*, June 27, 1960, 80. https://books.google.com/books?id=hR8EAAAAMBAJ.
65. "Know Your Suppliers." *Journal of the American Pharmaceutical Association* NS10, no. 8 (August 1970): 470-73.
66. Kobrak, Christopher. *National Cultures and International Competition: The Experience of Schering AG, 1851-1950.* Cambridge University Press, 2002.
67. Koenig, David. *The 55ers: The Pioneers Who Settled Disneyland.* Irvine: Bonaventure Press, 2019.
68. Korkis, Jim. "The Story of the Upjohn Pharmacy at Disneyland." MousePlanet. May 11, 2016. Accessed September 25, 2020. https://www.mouseplanet.com/11400/The_Story_of_the_Upjohn_Pharmacy_at_Disneyland.
69. Kravetz, Robert E. *Hucksters, Healers and Heroes: Medicine in Territorial Arizona, an Exhibition, Arizona Hall of Fame Museum, State of Arizona Department of Library Archives and Public Records, October 1, 1993—June 30, 1996.* Phoenix, AZ: Arizona Hall of Fame Museum, 1996.
70. Kravetz, Robert E., and Alex Jay Kimmelman. *Healthseekers in Arizona.* Phoenix, AZ: Academy of Medical Sciences of Maricopa Medical Society, 1998.
71. "Legislation and Judicial Decisions of Interest to Pharmacists for the Year 1901-1902." *The American Journal of Pharmacy* (July 1902): 336. https://search.proquest.com/docview/89682224.
72. Liberty, John. "Read These Seldom-seen Letters from Walt Disney to Donald Gilmore, Founder of the Gilmore Car Museum." MLive, August 2, 2014. Accessed March 26, 2018. http://www.mlive.com/entertainment/kalamazoo/index.ssf/2014/08/read_these_letters_from_walt_d.html.
73. Liberty, John. "Walt Disney in Kalamazoo: Filmmaker's Visit Among Milestones at Gilmore Car Museum." MLive, August 2, 2014. Accessed March 28, 2018. http://www.mlive.com/entertainment/kalamazoo/index.ssf/2014/08/walt_disney_in_kalamazoo_filmm.html
74. Light, Richard Upjohn, Alan Rowland Kiddle, and Michael Philip Upjohn. *Upjohn: A Study in Ancestry.* 1st ed. Vol. 1. 2 vols. Kalamazoo, MI: Richard Upjohn Light, 1990.

75. "Main Street Apothacary [*sic*] Shop Turn-of-Century Recreation." ***The Disneyland News***, November 1955.
76. "Marceline's Grave Robber." ***St. Louis Post-Dispatch***, March 21, 1895.
77. Marr, Luther. "Lease Brief." Disneyland, Inc., 1955.
78. Mason, Dave. ***The Little Shop on Main Street (The History of Ruggles China and Glass Shop)***. Blurb, 2014.
79. McKeever, Michael A. "EEEU! YUCK! LEECHES!" Old Guy New Blog (blog). March 13, 2012. https://oldguynewblog.tumblr.com/post/19242289374/eeeu-yuck-leeches.
80. ***Merck's Report*** 6, no. 4 (1897): 134.
81. Mobley, J. ***Prescription for Success: The Chain Drug Story***. Hallmark Cards, Inc., 1990.
82. Monsanto Hall of Chemistry brochure. St. Louis, MO: Monsanto Chemical Company.
83. "Museum Exhibits Record Pharmacy's Heritage.'" ***Journal of the American Pharmaceutical Association*** 21, no. 8 (1960): 488. https://www.japha.org/article/S0003-0465(15)30742-4/pdf
84. Nadel, Leonard. 1955 (photograph). The Upjohn Pharmacy Collection, Coit Museum of Pharmacy & Health Sciences, The University of Arizona, Tucson, AZ.
85. Nathoo, Ayesha. "Your Life in Your Hands: Teaching 'relaxed Living' in Post-war Britain." In ***Balancing the Self: Medicine, Politics and the Regulation of Health in the Twentieth Century***. Manchester: Manchester University Press, 2020.
86. ***National Druggist*** 25, no. 4 (1895): 63.
87. Nelson, Gary L. ***Pharmaceutical Company Histories***. Vol. 1. Bismarck, ND: Woodbine Pub., 1983.
88. Neuman, Robert. "Disneyland's Main Street, USA, and Its Sources in Hollywood, USA." ***The Journal of American Culture*** 31, no. 1 (2008).
89. "New Century Clock Shop." D23: The Official Disney Fan Club. Accessed March 30, 2018. https://d23.com/a-to-z/new-century-clock-shop/.
90. Nichols, J. J. "Merchandising U.S.P. Products" ***Journal of the American Pharmaceutical Association*** 20, no. 11 (November 1931): 1187. https://www.sciencedirect.com/science/article/abs/pii/S0898140X15378861?via%3Dihub.
91. "No Fantasy: Upjohn Found In Disneyland." ***The Intercom***. September 1986.
92. "Now That the Full Story Can Be Told." ***Upjohn News***, July 1946, pp. 3-5.
93. O'Reilly, Colleen. "Science, Politics, and Visual Design in Cold War America: Will Burtin's 'Cell.'" ***Visual Resources*** (2018).
94. Odell, Mark. "Schering Defends Its Record." CNNMoney. February 24, 1999. Accessed August 05, 2020. https://money.cnn.com/1999/02/24/europe/schering/.
95. Orvell, Miles. ***The Death and Life of Main Street: Small Towns in American Memory, Space, and Community***. Chapel Hill: University of North Carolina Press, 2012: 37-42, 241.
96. Parfet, Martha Gilmore. ***Keep the Quality Up***. Martha Gilmore Parfet, 2015.
97. Peterson, Arthur F. ***Pharmaceutical Selling, "Detailing," and Sales Training***. Scarsdale, NY: Heathcote-Woodbridge, 1949. (As quoted in Greene 2004.)
98. "Pharmacia Merger." Pfizer. Accessed May 02, 2021. https://www.pfizer.com/about/history/pfizer_pharmacia.
99. Pierce, Todd James. ***Three Years in Wonderland: The Disney Brothers, C.V. Wood, and the Making of the Great American Theme Park***. Jackson: University Press of Mississippi, 2016.
100. Pratt, W. D. ***The Abbott Almanac: 100 Years of Commitment to Quality Health Care***. Elmsford, NY: Benjamin, 1988.
101. Radcliff, Shirley to Richard Wiedhopf. September 27, 2007. California Science Center, Los Angeles, California.
102. Redpath, Frederick Lawrence. ***A String in the Fabric: The Story of the Upjohn Family***. Kalamazoo, MI: Richard U. Light, 1975.
103. Remington, R. Roger, and Robert S. P. Fripp. ***Design and Science: The Life and Work of Will Burtin***. Lund Humphries, 2007.

104. "Research Inquiry." Series of emails between Michael Wells (Kansas City Public Library) and author. July 2020.
105. Roberson, W. G. to R. T. Parfet Jr. September 24, 1970.
106. Roe, Jason. "Katz in the Cradle." KC History. Accessed August 06, 2020. https://kchistory.org/week-kansas-city-history/katz-cradle.
107. Royle, Robert W. *Upjohn Advertising Then and Now: A Combined Case History and Case Study of the Advertising of the Upjohn Company of Kalamazoo, Michigan.* Master's thesis. East Lansing: Michigan State University, 1964.
108. Rozenkier v. Schering AG & Bayer AG, 334 F. Supp. 2d 690, 694 (D.N.J. 2004).
109. Sampson, Wade, and Bob Gurr. "Disney Legend Bob Gurr: Filling in the Gaps." MousePlanet. September 01, 2010. Accessed July 22, 2020. https://www.mouseplanet.com/9361/Disney_Legend_Bob_Gurr_Filling_in_the_Gaps.
110. Sayers, Jack C. to E. G. Upjohn. September 20, 1960.
111. "Schering AG History." FundingUniverse. Accessed July 24, 2020. http://www.fundinguniverse.com/company-histories/schering-ag-history/.
112. "Schering Corp Opens Healthland Exhibit.'" *Hospital Topics* 38, no. 10 (1960): 136. doi:
113. 10.1080/00185868.1960.9954455
114. "Second Progress Report: Upjohn in Disneyland." *The Overflow,* June 1955, 182-185.
115. "Set of (9) Main Street U.S.A. Architectural Drawings." Van Eaton Galleries. https://bid.vegalleries.com/Set-of-9-Main-Street-U-S-A-Architectural-Drawings_i40961898.
116. Smith, Dave. *Disney Trivia from the Vault: Secrets Revealed and Questions Answered.* New York: Disney Editions, 2012.
117. Smith, Mickey C. "Images of Pharmacy and Pharmacists in Old-Time Radio: A Profile of Richard Q. Peavey." *Pharmacy in History* 25, no. 1 (1983): 19-29.
118. Smith, Mickey C. "Pharmacy and Radio: 1935-1960." *Pharmacy in History* 32, no. 1 (1990): 22-25.
119. Smith, Mickey C. and Steve Kremer. "Fibber McGee and Kremer's Drugstore." *Pharmacy in History* 50, no. 3 (2008): 119-124.
120. Smith, Mickey C. *The Rexall Story: A History of Genius and Neglect.* Binghamton, NY: Pharmaceutical Products Press, 2005.
121. Smothers, Marcy. *Eat like Walt: The Wonderful World of Disney Food.* Los Angeles: Disney Editions, 2017.
122. "So Dear to My Heart: Aunt Margaret." The Walt Disney Family Museum. September 08, 2011. Accessed July 13, 2020. https://www.waltdisney.org/blog/so-dear-my-heart-aunt-margaret.
123. Sonnedecker, Glenn, David L. Cowen, and Gregory Higby. *Drugstore Memories: American Pharmacists Recall Life Behind the Counter, 1824-1933.* Madison, WI: American Institute of the History of Pharmacy, 2002.
124. Strickland, William A. *The Apothecary Trail in Greater Kansas City, 1885-1985: The First 100 Years of Pharmaceutical Education.* Kansas City, MO: University of Missouri-Kansas City, School of Pharmacy, 1985.
125. Sturr, Henry. Upjohn Pharmacy in Disneyland [Memo]. September 25, 1970.
126. Taylor, Alan. "Opening Day at Disneyland: Photos From 1955." *The Atlantic.* July 24, 2019.
127. "The Cell Goes to Disneyland." (Unknown Upjohn publication.)
128. *The Disney Theme Show: From Disneyland to Walt Disney World, A Pocket History of the First Twenty Years. Vol. 1.* Los Angeles: Walt Disney Productions, 1976. (As cited in Wallace 1996, 136.)
129. *The Disneyland News,* November 1956.
130. *The First Ten Years of the World Health Organization.* Geneva: World Health Organization, 1958.
131. "The Organization Within the Organization: Upjohn Company..." *Disneylander,* September 1958, 2-3.
132. *The Pharmaceutical Era* 13 (June 27, 1895): 819.
133. "The Time Before Clocks." *Disneyland Line,* May 1, 1992: 2-3.
134. "The Upjohn Company at 100: Good Medicine for Its Community

and the World." ***Encore: Magazine of the Arts***, April 1986.
135. "The Upjohn Pharmacy in Disneyland." ***Scope***, Winter 1955.
136. "The Upjohn Pharmacy: A Showplace Within a Showplace." ***The Overflow***, November 1955, 402-404.
137. Thinnes, Tom. "Disney in Kalamazoo." ***Museography*** 6, no, 3. Kalamazoo Valley Museum, 2007. https://www.kalamazoomuseum.org/info/museON/museographies/Muse_XVIII.pdf.
138. "Third Progress Report: The Grand Opening." ***The Overflow***, September 1955, 331-333.
139. "This Week's Calendar." ***The Los Angeles Times***, October 13, 1963. https://www.proquest.com/historical-newspapers/other-5-no-title/docview/168450077/se-2.
140. "To Branch Out—Four Stores of Druggist Incorporated for Quarter Million." ***The Brookville Democrat***, July 29, 1914.
141. Tomes, Nancy. "The Great American Medicine Show Revisited." ***Bulletin of the History of Medicine*** 79, no. 4 (2005): 627-63. https://doi.org/10.1353/bhm.2005.0173.
142. "Touch of Petaluma in Disneyland." ***Petaluma Argus-Courier***, January 8, 1958.
143. Trahan, Kendra, Brian McKim, Karl Yamauchi, Dave Hawkins, and Debbie Smith. ***Disneyland Detective: An Independent Guide to Discovering Disney's Legend, Lore and Magic***. Mission Viejo: PermaGrin Publishing, 2015.
144. Tremblay, Christopher W. ***Walt's Pilgrimage: A Journey in the Life of Walter Elias Disney***. United States: Christopher W. Tremblay, 2017.
145. "Triangle of Health: Keeping the Balance (film)." D23: The Official Disney Fan Club. Accessed April 30, 2020. https://d23.com/a-to-z/triangle-of-health-keeping-the-balance-film/
146. U.S. Census Bureau. "Missouri: Number and Distribution of Inhabitants." 1920. Accessed June 10, 2020. https://www2.census.gov/prod2/decennial/documents/06229686v20-25ch4.pdf.
147. Uchitelle, Louis. "Aiming at H.M.O.'s, Upjohn Agrees to $13 Billion Merger." ***The New York Times***, August 21, 1995. Accessed May 2, 2021. https://www.nytimes.com/1995/08/21/business/aiming-at-hmo-s-upjohn-agrees-to-13-billion-merger.html.
148. "Upjohn & Disney's Triangle of Health." YouTube video, 52:28. Posted August 2018. https://www.youtube.com/watch?v=QT5Sp-foN4&t=16s.
149. ***Upjohn Annual Report—1959***. Ann Arbor: ProQuest Annual Reports, 1959. https://www.proquest.com/reports/upjohn-annual-report-1959/docview/88192800/se-2.
150. ***Upjohn Annual Report—1966***. Ann Arbor: ProQuest Annual Reports, 1966. https://www.proquest.com/reports/upjohn-annual-report-1966/docview/88198783/se-2.
151. "Upjohn Company to Operate 1890s Drugstore at Disneyland." ***The Carolina Journal of Pharmacy*** 36, no. 4 (1955): 163. https://dc.lib.unc.edu/cdm/ref/collection/nchh/id/1003157.
152. "Upjohn contacts." Series of emails between David Koenig and author. November 2020.
153. "Upjohn Disneyland Items." Email from George MacLeod to Richard Wiedhopf. June 30, 2014.
154. "Upjohn Disneyland Material." Series of emails between Lynn Houghton (Western Michigan University Archives) and author. July 2019.
155. "Upjohn Disneyland Pharmacy Collection." Series of emails between Luke Fernandez (California Science Center) and author. 2018-2019.
156. "Upjohn in Disneyland." ***The Overflow***, April 1955, 113-119.
157. "Upjohn Name Missing From Disneyland." ***The Kalamazoo Gazette***, December 27, 1970.
158. "Upjohn Pharmacy." D23: The Official Disney Fan Club. Accessed March 30, 2018. https://d23.com/a-to-z/upjohn-pharmacy/.
159. "Upjohn Pharmacy at Disney—Chalk Painting." Series of emails between Dale Erick Rush (University of Illinois at Chicago) and author. September/October 2019.
160. "Upjohn Pharmacy in Disneyland." Series of emails between Brittany Williams (Kalamazoo Valley Museum) and author. August 2019.

161. *Upjohn Pharmacy Photograph.* August 4, 1955. Disney History 101.
162. Upjohn Pharmacy Postcard. Kalamazoo, MI: Upjohn Company.
163. Upjohn, E. G. to Marian Ganong. July 5, 1955.
164. Urdang, George, and Edward Kremers. *History of Pharmacy.* Philadelphia: J.B. Lippincott Company, 1946.
165. Vilz, Amy. *Will Burtin Papers, C.1857-1972 (bulk 1955-1972).* December 2000. Will Burtin Finding Aid, Rochester Institute of Technology, Rochester, NY.
166. Virgintino, Michael R. *Freedomland U.S.A.: The Definitive History.* Theme Park Press, 2019.
167. *Walgreens: Celebrating 100 Years as the Pharmacy America Trusts.* Deerfield, IL: Walgreen Co., 2001.
168. Wallace, Mike. *Mickey Mouse History: The Politics of Public Memory.* USA: Temple University Press, 1996: 134-138.
169. "Western Union Telegram, 7:44 AM." Marian Ganong to E. G. Upjohn. July 2, 1955. Walt Disney Studios, Burbank, CA.
170. "Will Burtin 'The Cell,'" "Upjohn Disneyland Photos," etc. Multiple series of emails between Jeremy Winkworth and author. 2014-2019.
171. *Wisdom*, December 1959. (As quoted in Watts 1997, pg. 22 and Francaviglia 1996, pg. 153.)
172. "Wood, C. V., Jr." D23: The Official Disney Fan Club. Accessed July 22, 2020. https://d23.com/a-to-z/wood-c-v-jr/.

Page numbers in *italics* indicate illustrations.

N

O

P